R.K. Jensen

What others are saying about R.K. Jensen's story:

"As a Pastor for thirty years I have seen many of God's miracles and I can tell you this is one of them. It is my prayer that teens and pre-teens, as well as any adult involved in a young person's life will see how God can work miracles in all of our lives."

Pastor Arthur C. Fisher
Canyon Community Nazarene, Corona, CA

"R.K. Jensen is a testament to the power of faith and determination to go beyond mere survival of severe child abuse, parental neglect, as well as drug and alcohol addiction, and to keep pursuing our dreams. His story is an inspiration to us all and sheds great insight for professionals and other concerned adults who make it their aim to work with today's at-risk youth."

Kathy Silbert-Sanders, Ph.D., L.C.S.W.
Psychiatric Social Worker,
Los Angeles County Department of Mental Health

"Teens will really be inspired by this book. This amazing story shows how your surroundings don't create who you are. It doesn't matter what your background is; you can always make an amazing life for yourself and see that almost anything you dream of becoming can come true. Anyone can do it. Dreams are not just for those with a "fairy-tale" life, but also for kids who grow up hurting."

Erin Sanders, Professional Teen Actress

"This is one man's story but it is the story of thousands of youth in our country involved in gangs. This book sheds light on an intervention so often overlooked: spirituality. God can have a profound effect on people from all walks of life by bringing a sense of hope, focus, and self-awareness. God does not turn His back on anyone, not even gang bangers."
Lisa Taylor-Austin, MS Ed., NCC, LPC
Forensic Gang Expert Witness/Psychotherapist
www.gangcolors.com

"Mr. Jensen, I would like to tell you that your book, *Left for Dead - Faith, Family, & the Mob*, has touched something inside me I didn't believe was there. Sir, I served in the United States Marine Corps and I've seen and been through some terrible things. As a POW (Prisoner of War) in Iran I learned how to truly hate people. I'm in jail for *(private)* and I'm not sure what is going to happen yet. I do know that your book has made me want a relationship with God."
R.D.P. *(Identity protected)*, **Retired U.S. Marine**
Above Quotation taken from a personal letter sent to the author.

ಸಂ R.K. JENSEN ରେ

FORWARD

"R.K. Jensen has written a powerful story of a powerful life... a life begun in the low-income, crime ridden streets of the Los Angeles area. Yet, the story doesn't end there.

Jensen truly captivates the reader with a story *well told* of struggle, defeat and ultimate triumph. Each of us needs encouragement. R.K. Jensen's book touches the soul, gives life to the heart and refreshes the spirit. *You can't get better than that in any book!*

Read it; share it with friends of *all* economic levels. Give it to a youth who is struggling. Share it with a businessman who needs encouragement or a homemaker who needs guidance with her kids.

Jensen's life story is a triumph of God's will ~ from which I have seen one man's success come from an upbringing full of defeat. May you enjoy this story as I have. May you be fortunate to meet the author and see his life in full bloom, as I also have.

R.K. Jensen has written this generation's new biography of a different type of 'switchblade' while still under the shadow of the same old rugged 'cross'."

Dennis Mansfield
Speaker, CBS Commentator (KBCI TV), Founder/CEO
of Focus on the Family's Family Policy Council, in Boise, Idaho
Founder, Promise Keepers Radio; State Director, Promise Keepers, Idaho

3

LEFT FOR DEAD
Faith, Family, and the Mob

R.K. JENSEN

www.aaroncom3.com

ഔ R.K. Jensen ଓ

Published by:
Aaron Communications III
P.O. Box 63270
Colorado Springs, CO 80962-3270

Publication date: September 15, 2006
Copyright 2006, R.K. Jensen
All rights reserved.
Printed in Canada.
The Library of Congress Cataloging-in-Publication Data:
Jensen, R.K.
Left for dead : faith, family, and the mob / R.K. Jensen.
p. cm.
ISBN 0-9763964-1-6 (hc.)
ISBN 0-9763964-0-8 (sc.)
ISBN 0-9763964-2-4 (Acrobat E-Book)
2005922052

Photo of R.K. Jensen: Jane Hunt Photography, Hollywood, CA
Cover Graphic Design, and layout: R.K. Jensen
The Window Boy photo: Adam Sablich.
Cover photo of boy with brown eyes: Karen Black (www.blackeye.com.au)
Cover photo of boy with blue eyes: Sally Bradshaw. Each used by permission.
"Scripture quotations taken from the New American Standard Bible(r),
Copyright (c) 1960, 1962, 1963, 1968, 1971, 1972, 1973,
1975, 1977, 1995 by The Lockman Foundation
Used by permission." (www.Lockman.org)

Without limiting the rights under copyright reserved above, no part of this publication may be reproduced, stored in or introduced into a retrieval system, or transmitted, in any form, or by any means (electronic, mechanical, photocopying, recording, or otherwise), without the prior written permission of both the copyright owner and the above publisher of this book.

PUBLISHERS NOTE:

The scanning, uploading, and distribution of this book via the Internet or via any other means without the permission of the publisher is illegal and punishable by law. Please purchase only authorized electronic editions, and do not participate in or encourage electronic piracy of copyrighted materials. Your support of the author's rights is appreciated.

QUANTITY DISCOUNTS ARE AVAILABLE WHEN USED TO PROMOTE PRODUCTS, SERVICES, OR MINISTRIES. FOR INFORMATION PLEASE WRITE TO THE SPECIALTY DIVISION OF AARON COMMUNICATIONS III AT ABOVE ADDRESS.

DEDICATION

Every key stroke, every page written, every chapter of this book was lovingly written in dedication to the memory of my first-born son Ronnie Keith. "Son, you touched our lives with the peace of God Almighty, and taught your mom and I what truly matters most in this life."

I also dedicate this book to the memory of my two brothers Bobby and Jeff. Bobby, as a child you looked after Jeff and I when our parents abandoned us to the mean streets of Southern California, and to Jeff, my younger brother, my heart breaks for you, and for the loss that we all shared.

Most of all to the most precious gifts in my life: to my wife Anne and to our children Seth, Audrey, and Natalie. God has truly blessed your mom and me with more than we could have ever hoped for.

ഔ R.K. Jensen ര

IMPORTANT AUTHOR'S NOTES

Concerning children: Some of the subject matter in this book is described in graphic detail, yet without offensive language, making it necessary to ask parents and youth-workers to please consider the age level of the children or youth who read this book. The overall consensus of Clergy and Youth Professionals is the age-appropriate-level is for ten-year-olds on up (depending on the childs maturity level) to the teen level, as well as offering a great deal of insight to adults concerned with today's youth.

Character & truth disclosure/release: I have changed the names of those in my past who are living and who continue to live in urban areas to shield their identities because this is a true story about the mob and actual California gangs, most of which are still active today. Every event written herein is true and factual, having been verified by different sources (see commentaries), there are no half truth's or exaggerations of any sort. I have kept my name in the book so that you would know this is a true story in every detail. Lastly, the book was purposely written at the middle school age level so that all youth can understand and gain from reading this book, while at the same time staying true to the story so the story remains relevant for older teens and adults. I sincerely hope this message of hope and triumph will inspire all who read these pages, and I encourage you to share this story with others. I especially encourage youth or adults concerned with youth to correspond via email or traditional mail with any comments or questions that you may have. I will respond personally to your letter.

Thank you so very much for your support,

R.K. Jensen

Publishers Note: "Please mail all correspondence directly to Publisher, your letter will be delivered to the author."

Aaron Communications III
Re: R.K. Jensen
P.O. Box 63270
Colorado Springs, CO 80962

Or e-mail to: aaroncom3rkjensen@yahoo.com

Contents

FORWARD	3
PROLOGUE	12
RAISED BY THE MOB	17
ABANDONED	27
RIOT	49
PROMISE KEPT	68
SEPARATE ROADS	82
BEYOND BELIEF	93
BLOOD BETRAYAL	110
HIGHER GROUND	119
FORGIVENESS	135
RETURN OF THE MOB	145
PLANS FOR GOOD	160
AFTERWARD	174
EPILOGUE	179
KEYNOTES	180
FREE BOOKS PROGRAM	182
APPENDIX A: GOD'S PLAN	185
INSPIRATIONAL ART	198

LEFT FOR DEAD

Faith, Family, and the Mob

R.K. Jensen

PROLOGUE

Southern California Ghetto, September 1980

Snoop, Freddie, and I were walking down the middle of State Street talking about what a bad evening it had been, not realizing the worst was yet to come. In the meantime three gangsters from the 12th Street Sharkey's gang were on their way to carry out plans for revenge against the Earth Angel's gang. They sent three of their deadliest adult gang members to carry out the assassination plan. The quickest way for the Sharks to get to the Earth Angel's territory was to drive straight down State Street.

The three of us teenaged street kids were so buzzed from the alcohol we couldn't feel the cold of the night. I felt like we were walking in slow motion, as though time had stopped for that moment. That is when we noticed the round headlights coming from behind us. We moved over to the side of the road next to an abandoned strawberry field, only blocks away from Snoops' house. On the other side of the street you could see the black silhouette of the train cars and of the grain mills.

It was totally silent, as though the oncoming car had no running engine. The car pulled over to the side right in front of Snoop and Freddie. It was a Gold-toned 1969 Chevy Impala Low-rider, with a crack in the windshield. Inside were three adult gang members. Snoop and Freddie talked to them for what seemed to be forever. Snoop and

Freddie backed down from representing their hometown, then backed away from the car.

"What gang are you from?" I heard the shout come from inside of the 1969 Chevy Impala. I had been taught by the toughest of the gangsters from the Earth Angel's gang to back down from no one. I could vaguely see the three gangsters inside. Without hesitation I stood my ground and responded, "Earth Angel's rule!" Immediately out of nowhere a beer bottle came flying at my face, cutting my nose open.

Snoop yelled, "He's got a gun!" We ran in the opposite direction of the car. It was at that moment we heard the gunshots. Blam, Blam, Blam. One shot right after another. As I ran I could feel the hot bullets piercing the flesh on my back. Blam. Another searing hot bullet pierced my back.

At that point I looked behind me to see Snoop and Freddie both hit the ground. I followed suit and fell to the ground, hoping the shooting would stop. Everything was happening in split second timing. I looked behind me hoping to see the taillights of my attackers' car driving away. Instead I saw one of the gangsters getting out of the low rider car. I heard a shout, "get his sweater!"

I realized he was coming to take the sweater off of my back, the sweater that had my gangs' logo and name on it. The Earth Angel's logo was the image of Death waving a sickle over the earth. I immediately started running into the dark abandoned field. Blam, Blam. More shots were fired. I could feel another bullet pierce my back, then, another. I was a goner for sure now, yet I couldn't give up. I kept running with my attacker in hot pursuit. I looked behind me only to see the gangster pulling out a switchblade knife. Looking ahead I came to a chain-link fence. I began to claw at the fence, trying to get over the top, as I watched Snoop and Freddie jump over the top as an athlete jumps over a hurdle.

I froze at the top of the fence with my arm stretched out toward Snoop and Freddie I yelled into the dark night, "Snoop, Freddie, heeeelp meeee!", as they disappeared into the darkness, not once turning back. Within seconds my attacker caught up to me and began stabbing my left leg. I let go of my grasp of the fence and fell to the ground headfirst. The blow to my head knocked me out cold. As I lie there he repeatedly stabbed me well over fifteen times - all over my body. I regained consciousness only to find him kicking me in the face with his steel-toed shoes. He was trying to pull off my sweater. Finally, I raised my arms to let the sweater go.

"Where is he?" shouted the gangster with the gun from the end of the field, where the gold-toned Low Rider sit. "He's over here, I got his sweater." Within seconds the gangster with the gun was standing over me pointing the gun at my head. I could feel the bullet pierce through my skin, through my skull, and into my brain, before he pulled that trigger, as he stood there aiming for my forehead. I knew this was it. This would be the final blow. If he pulled the trigger, there was no surviving this shot. His job was to make for certain that I was dead.

Before he could pull that trigger I had to have one last chance at hope. I couldn't watch him blow my head off. I put my bloodied left arm over my eyes and did something that touched the inner-most part of this man's darkened soul as he was about to end the life of a fourteen-year old without even a second thought. With my eyes closed and

covered with my bloodied arm, blood and tears running down my cheek, knowing within seconds he'd pull the trigger, I did the sign of the cross. I moved my left hand and touched my forehead, then moved my hand over my heart, then to my right shoulder, finally to my left shoulder, ending with a kiss to God. The gangster threw his head back and said, "Woe, you believe in God?" Quickly I replied, "Yes"...
(To be continued in the chapter entitled "Riot")

Over the last few decades countless thousands of youth in the United States of America, and around the world, have been violently beaten and murdered by the mafia, gangs, and sadly at the hands of a parent. These lost lives have gone unnoticed; forgotten, and abandoned young souls, young flames of life snuffed out in the dark night. Life violently ripped from them - before ever having a fair chance at life.

Following is the true-life story of two such lives.

R.K. JENSEN

RAISED BY THE MOB

The earliest memories I have of my family date back to 1969, when I was just three-years-old, we were living in Montclair, California, about twenty-five miles east of Los Angeles. The part of town we lived in was a pretty decent neighborhood. Swimming Pools and make-believe forts filled the back yards. Hard working middle income families lived here. Through the eyes of the kids everything seemed pretty normal. I remember Christmas time most of all.

Christmas filled the air. Our whole family went together to pick out the biggest Christmas tree on the Christmas tree lot. The unforgettable smell of a fresh evergreen tree, mixed with the smell of baked Christmas cookies and cakes. We took turns lacing the popcorn onto a string to make a garland, to wrap around the nicely decorated tree. Afterwards we watched the Christmas specials on television with a serving of ice cream. Grandma and Grandpa were there to watch over us while mom and dad were out shopping. Finally, dad would pick me up and lift me to the top of the tree to add the finishing touch, the brilliantly colored star that topped the magical Christmas tree.

Christmas morning was the best of all. Knowing Santa had visited and left every gift our hearts had desired. I remember waking up Christmas morning, my brothers and I ran down stairs to see a large pile of Christmas presents under the tree, or actually, underneath, and flowing over to the middle of the living room. My sister Helen, the oldest of the bunch, received games and dolls. Bobby my older brother got a new bike, along with tons of other presents. Jeff, the youngest of the boys, he was only two, was happy to get stuffed animals. I got a sit-'n-spin, along with tons of other great stuff. There were more gifts than we knew what to do with.

Through the eyes of innocent children life seemed normal. These were happy times for my family. However, unknown to my sister, brothers, and I, this happy life was in direct contrast to the dark reality of mob life that my parents were heavily involved in.

It was during this time in our lives that there came a loud knock at the front door of our home. I opened the door to find a swarm of police officers. "Hello," said the police officer "is your daddy home?" I responded the best way a three-year-old knew how by saying, "sure he is, he's inside making money, isn't that great!" The police pulled me out of the house onto the patio, and then went inside our home. I honestly don't remember what happened after the police put me outside. I learned much later that my dad was hauled off to Federal Prison for counterfeiting twenty-dollar bills for the mob. Our parents were able to afford everything as a result of doing various assignments for the mob. My dad had been a member of what is called the Arian Brotherhood, the white mob, since his teen days.

Dad grew up in Rancho Cucamonga, California, with his mom and a step-dad. Back then Cucamonga was mostly made up of vineyards and wineries. Down the street from grandma's house, on Haven and Foothill Blvd, was what seemed to be an ancient abandoned winery with a stream running nearby. My grandfather raised him as his own. Dad didn't have any brothers or sisters. Not counting the two foster kids his mom took in. Dad left home at the age of sixteen, ending up in East Los Angeles. Although he moved to a mixed neighborhood of Latinos and Caucasians, he got along with the Latinos of East Los Angeles. They gave him the nickname Blade. He learned a lot about motorbikes and the way of the streets. He became as they say in the inner cities "street smart". He had a lot of scuffs with the law. It wasn't too long before he'd end up with the men who made up the beginning of what is now known as the Arian Brotherhood, the "AB" for short. The AB was a step up for Blade. He had hung with the bikers, and the gangsters. Now Blade was a full-fledged member of organized crime.

The AB is Nation-wide and is operated within and outside of the prison system. Members of the AB own several businesses, and yet are still heavily involved in drug trafficking, gambling, and prostitution. They control a large portion of the drug market in America from coast to coast. Blade was not a higher up in the AB. Yet he knew all the right people and had all the right connections. I am not saying anything about the AB that isn't common knowledge to the police or F.B.I., or to anyone who knows a little something about the white mob. Anyone can visit the F.B.I.'s web site covering the AB. My dad never involved us in any super secret illegal activities of the mob. For the most part he kept it outside of the home (I suppose he learned his lesson with the counterfeiting: keep it away from the family!).

My mom, Marie L. Garcia, grew up with her four sisters in nearby Ontario. Both of her parents had passed away when mom was a child. Mom was only 5 when her mother died as a result of an automobile accident. Her dad died of a heart attack when she was fifteen-years old.

My parents met in Upland after my dad moved back from Los Angeles, soon after they wed in Las Vegas,

Nevada. Their marriage was rough from the start. Mom had my older sister Helen from a previous relationship. Blade became involved in everything the mob had to offer, from committing armed robbery, to running drugs from Mexico and Canada into the U.S.A.

In 1964 my parents had their first-born son who they named Robert, we called him Bobby. I came along a little over a year later in 1966. Bobby got all of my dad's features of a light complexion, blue eyes, and light brown hair. I got my mom's coloration of olive skin, black hair, and brown eyes. During this time Blade hung out with bikers. These men were members of the Arian Brotherhood. It was during this time that Blade pulled armed robberies, dealed drugs, and took trips to Mexico to smuggle drugs back to the Los Angeles area in his brand new '69 Chevy Impala painted in pearl white with black leather seats.

In the late sixties my parents were leasing a restaurant inside of a bar. Mom was trying to make it work. From what I've been told my mom made the best chili in all of Southern California. Blade served as the bouncer but also used it as an opportunity to deal drugs. The whole thing ended when he robbed the bar they were leasing the restaurant from.

Sometime later Blade was given a set of printing plates and a small printing press. The plates were of twenty-dollar bills. The counterfeit money was to be used to purchase drugs from other mob groups. Another use of counterfeit money would be to sell large amounts of the phony cash for smaller amounts of real cash.

It seemed my parents had a way of ruining things for each other. My mom took several twenties from the counterfeit pile without my dad's knowledge. She then took the counterfeit money and had her girl friend trade it for real money from her husband's wallet, without her husband's knowledge. The two ladies then went on a shopping spree.

Sometime thereafter, her friend's husband was arrested for distributing counterfeit money. His wife, through tears in her eyes, explained to the F.B.I. what happened. That is when I was at the age of three the police came knocking on our door late at night to carry my dad away.

With my dad gone we had to move to a different city. The house was much smaller in an area known as the ghetto, or the inner city. We called it "the hood". The house was painted sky blue and had a small chain link fence around it. Across the street was an abandoned field overgrown with weeds. We were near the corner, by a busy street where the people drove recklessly. Within months of our living there a mother would lose her newborn child to one of these reckless drivers. She was simply pushing her baby in a stroller across the narrow road. The speeding car came out of nowhere, without warning narrowly missing the mother, running over the stroller with the baby still inside. This marked the beginning of a very dark time in our childhood, as we would become aware over time of the effects mob life would have on our family.

Blade was released from Federal Prison within three years. After his release he spent a lot of time away from home. Some shady looking people began coming over. I noticed as well we were starting to have nice things again. We all had brand new bikes, a swimming pool in the back yard, and nice gifts for the holidays. This time it wasn't quite the same. Something felt wrong.

My dad became abusive toward my mom. I remember her screams coming out of their bedroom, as my two brothers and I ran in to see my dad on top of her, slugging her as if he were in a brawl with a man. We jumped on dad's back, as he reached around his back to move us off he gave my seven-year old brother Bobby a black eye. That ended the fight, but things just kept going bad for Blade.

It turned out he was pimping prostitutes. Instead of spending the money he gained from selling the prostitutes, he laundered it through a furniture store. The F.B.I. was on to him and Blade knew he didn't have an out. According to a relative, I learned that after being approached by the law, he agreed to turn States evidence against the furniture storeowner for laundering illegal money and for tax evasion. It was a business assassination. Blade once told me the best way to hurt an enemy that is worse than death is to ruin them financially in every way possible. Now he had a mob family after him. He figured the only safety was the covering of the Arian Brotherhood inside of the prison system. He hatched a plan to escape the mob family he turned on. To get his ticket to prison he stole a car and then broke into a business. After loading the car up with the stolen merchandise he sat there and fell asleep until the police arrived. While in prison he watched over a young inmate whose dad was a mob boss in the Italian Mafia. He made sure no one messed with him, granting him the protection of the Arian Brotherhood. This would prove handy to Blade because after he was released he would have a top position waiting for him with a major construction company on the East Coast, nearby New York. In the mob, favors are never done for free.

My mom filed for a divorce. She said it was the last straw. She couldn't take it anymore. What could any of us say? At the time none of us knew what he had done, or why he was gone. To us kids, he was dad. We didn't know anything of the mob and the dealings that were taking place. He even treated Helen and Jeff as though they were his own children. Life through the eyes of a child, and the love that child has for a parent knows no bounds, socially or economically. To any young child, a parent is just that, a mom or dad, regardless of the circumstances in the adult parent's life. Children do not know any different than the circumstances that they grow up in. To them it is what is normal. By this time I was only six years old. We were left with a sense of emptiness inside. The darkest part of my childhood had begun.

 Living in the ghetto was bad enough, now however, we moved to the worst part of town. We moved in the projects, in the heart of the ghetto. Small run-down apartments paid for by the government to some Slumlord. This was the spawning ground for future gang members and Mafia members.

 The change was too great. Helen, Bobby and I could all sense the change, something dying inside each one of us. My mom had changed as well. She would leave us at night to go out on dates. My sister was only ten or eleven at the time. We wouldn't see mom until the next morning. Terrible things would happen in the neighborhood, such as muggings, murder, vandalism, gang fights, and robberies.

 Prior to all this we were normal kids. Bobby would soon change drastically, as he started making friends from the new neighborhood. Bobby had to grow up too soon, as he had to be there for his younger brothers, Jeff and me.

I remember when we were kids Bobby was fun to be around. With all my parents put all of us through, we all felt safe when we were with him as kids. We'd always play board games together, as well as swim and go to the youth center to play games. He was athletic and strong. I even rode my first big carnival ride with him.

A traveling Carnival had come to the park across the street from the projects we lived in. The ride was called the Zipper. This contraption of a ride must have been two to four stories tall. It zipped you around, up and down and flipped you front-wards and backwards, seemingly all at the same time. I must have been about seven or eight years old. I wanted to be brave like him so I went on. I was so freaked out by the ride that the operator had to stop it to let the little kid who was crying off of the killer monster ride. I swore we were going to die up there. Bobby held my arm until I stopped crying, and didn't get mad at all. He was our big brother.

As a kid I had severe asthma, as a result I wasn't much of a fighter growing up. That made me a good target for kids wanting to prove their toughness to their friends. However, if anyone did touch me, not too long after Bobby would hunt the kid down and give him a good pounding. Bobby was a real natural visual artist.   He could draw, paint, and do calligraphy. I'm not talking about tagging or graffiti. He was talented in the true sense of the word. His art was the talk of the school. He would draw the most awesome Ocean themed drawings I had ever seen. I was a pretty good artist myself, following in his footsteps. We both won awards and recognition for our art. I was asked to paint the school mural in the Physical Ed room of the elementary school. He of course, was ahead of me with his talent. He watched out for us as best as could be expected. Our dad was no longer in our lives. We never visited him in jail, and when he left California, he never called, he only visited every other year or so as he was passing through on mob business. It was around this time that our mother met an alcoholic man at a bar. I don't know how long it was they had dated; yet it wasn't long before he moved in with us. He kept his job at the fish bait factory, while she remained on welfare. Rather than increase our standard of living and take care of our daily needs, mom and her live-in boyfriend kept us in the projects in the ghetto. The extra money brought in was used for endless parties with countless bottles of hard liquor, cases of beer, marijuana, gambling, and a brand new Turbo Pontiac Trans Am for him. My mom and her boy friend Ray Lopes got what they wanted, a little more for themselves.

  Helen, Bobby, Jeff, and I, Ron, took a back seat to my mother's new family: Ray, her live in boyfriend, and his family of sixteen brothers and sisters. Ray's brothers and sisters all lived in Pomona, the first city you come to in eastern Los Angeles County. Bobby and I were totally abandoned to the projects by our dad, and now our own mother had abandoned us altogether. The worst part about it is she abandoned us as young children while living under the same roof. The results and consequences of this lifestyle, of the mob, wild parties, and emotionally abandoning the kids, would be immediately seen in the lives of my sister, brothers, and I, living alone in our home in the days, weeks, and years to come.

ᛓ **R.K. Jensen** ᛕ

ABANDONED

It was late one Friday evening, in or around September of 1977. The strobe lights flashed on and off to the sound of loud music working everyone at the party into a frenzy as the drugs and booze were passed around freely. Empty beer bottles everywhere, plastic baggies filled with marijuana sitting on the table next to a small box of Zig Zag cigarette papers. The whole scene was like a wild adult party you would see in a rated R movie. Only the difference was this party was made up of mostly Junior High School kids and a couple of older teens. Marie and her live-in boyfriend Ray would return dead drunk at their usual time of about 4:00 a.m. in the morning.

The projects were run-down two story apartment buildings situated together forming a small community with a makeshift baseball field in the center where most of the kids got together during the day to play a rough game of baseball, pretending to be their favorite pro-baseball player. Many of these were the same kids that would come to the parties late at night at my place. I remember most of these kids from the projects. Sadly, many of them have since passed away. Falling victim to the gang violence they helped to create, it seemed the more a young person became involved the more they would lose their true identity, to include anything any one of us had ever hoped of becoming (yes, inner city youth have dreams and aspirations). Everyone received a nickname they would officially go by on the streets. Paul, my sister's boyfriend at the time, went by Psycho. Paul had a younger brother that was my age named Ricardo. Ricardo went by the street name Bandit. They lived in the projects with their single mom, only a few apartments away from us. Their dad was non-existent. Paul was truly crazy. In Junior High School, he and his younger brother Ricardo beat up the Principal in front of the entire school. Paul took part in many drive-by shootings, as did most of the gang members. What convinced me he was crazy was when he took his buck knife and stabbed himself in the stomach three or four times to see what it felt like.

There was a family from Mexico living right next door to us. Martin and his older brother Gary were clean-cut guys. Their dad was an immigrant who worked hard to provide for his family. Their mom spoke only Spanish. Gary and Martin managed to stay out of trouble for the time being. My younger brother Jeff and I were not involved in the gangs. We were exposed to them all of the time, especially because my mom left us to ourselves over the weekends. Jeff picked a nickname that was not in character with who he was; he picked Happy Boy. I went by the nickname Sleepy, as in one of the seven dwarfs in the Disney stories. I suppose Jeff longed for happiness, yet would be hard pressed to find it. At the time I was only eleven, and in the sixth grade, Jeff was only nine in the fourth grade.

My Aunt Alicia from my mother's side of the family lived nearby with her four children. Our oldest cousin Sal, along with his bully of a brother Doug, would come over all of the time. Their parents had been divorced as well. This was the one thing most of us project kids had in common, divorced parents, along with being abandoned either emotionally or outright abandoned by one or both

parents. These were the faces I'd see partying each and every weekend when our parents would abandon us to ourselves.
    Sal, our older cousin, was one of the first to join a gang. Only he didn't just join a gang, he was asked by the leaders of the Black Angels to start a Junior Gang in the neighborhood. The Black Angels gang originally started as the Red Devils in the late 1950's and the early 1960's. The name of the new gang would be called the Junior Black Angels. The junior version was used as a means to recruit and disciple young eleven-year olds on up to fifteen-year old Hispanic youth into the gang life, assuring the Black Angels fresh members for the future, replacing those who were murdered, paralyzed by gang violence, or in jail. Bobby and the rest were mad at Sal for joining ranks with the Black Angels. This became a common occurrence between family members and friends in our neighborhood. One brother would join the Black Angels; the other brother would join the Earth Angels gang (otherwise known as the EA's gang). Most all of the teens that had been partying at my house had joined the EA's gang, including Gary and Martin, my next door neighbors. Paul, a.k.a. Psycho, joined the Earth Angel's, while his younger brother Ricardo, a.k.a. Bandit, ended up joining the Jr. Black Angels.
    After a while some hard-core EA gang members I had never seen before started hanging around our place on the weekends. My brother Bobby was given the nickname Huero, which in Spanish means White Boy. Bobby stopped hanging around with our older cousin Sal, and became tight with Chato, the Vice President of the Earth Angel's, the neighborhood gang for our part of town. Chato was a

hard-core gang member who was at least 18 or 19 years of age. This is when Bobby joined the Earth Angel's gang. I would hear all about the trouble Bobby and Chato got into. I didn't see much of Bobby after that. I felt Chato and his gang took Bobby away from us. Bobby hooked up with some professional thieves out of Los Angeles who made it their business to stalk wealthy people's homes after watching for days at a time, taking only the most valuable possessions such as cash and jewels.

As the older teens became active members of the gangs, I, along with my younger cousin Doug, and my brother Jeff, began running the streets late at night and all hours of the day. Going to school only meant an opportunity to ditch and go to the mall to steal and hang around with the older gang members. Sal did a good job at teaching us how to steal from stores and how to break in houses. At any given hour of the day we were looking for ways to get into trouble. I remember this one-day in particular; I was in the eighth grade, and my younger brother Jeff was in the seventh grade.

We ditched school as usual and went to the nearby Shopping Mall. On the way to the mall we spotted several Marijuana plants growing in the side yard of some unknown person's house. Jeff and I got our book bags and loaded them up with the plants; saving them for later when we could bake the plant and smoke it up. While we were at the mall Jeff stole two men's watches from the jewelry case and then a realistic looking pellet gun from the sporting goods section at JC Penny's. I hate to say it, but stealing came natural to this kid.

On the way back to the school we decided to see if there were any more marijuana plants, so we jumped up onto the roof. Across the way on top of another home there were workers laying down shingles on a roof. I didn't notice until it was too late when Jeff took the pellet gun and pointed it at the workers, thinking he would be funny and act like he was doing a drive-by shooting. The workers jumped for their lives off the roof and didn't wait to take turns down the ladder. We ran back to the School. The cops found me in Art class and my brother on top of the gym roof. Jeff and I were taken to the Principals office and suspended for the incident. That was somewhat typical.

By the time I reached Middle School I had become like all the other troubled youth, yet I can honestly remember feeling like something had died inside of me. When I was a young kid, while all the other kids were playing sports and getting into trouble, I was reading, drawing, or even taking music lessons. I tried out for the sports teams, yet on account of having severe asthma I could not join. Even though I took medicine, it wasn't enough to keep me from nearly dying of asthma attacks. I had hopes of one day becoming a professional in the field of the Arts, or perhaps an actor. However, my parents never noticed. They wondered why I wasn't tough like all the other guys. My dad Blade even tried teaching me how to fist fight, but I declined.

As time went by I saw less of my parents. My dad was non-existent and by this time my mom had a son with Ray, her live-in boyfriend. I tried hard to get my mom's and even her boyfriend Ray's approval and support. All I received in return was neglect and abuse. Ray was physically and verbally abusive toward my sister, brothers, and me. Because I wasn't tough like the others I received the brunt of Ray's anger. I'm reminded of a time when I was only nine-years old. Ray got mad at me for tattling on the other kids, so he grabbed me by the throat and knocked me up against the door as he tightened his grip. That was pretty traumatic. My mom would get mad at him but say nothing. I felt so out of place. Nothing but sports and booze parties, drinking way past being drunk.

Ray was a big man, trained in karate, yet he did not stay true to the self-discipline aspects of the training. I still remember to this day when Ray karate kicked me out of my seat because I didn't want to go out to eat. I was only ten-years-old. Several times I'd see him beat my mom. One time out of nowhere, in front of his own mother and the kids, he reached over and karate punched my mom in the face, busting her lip and breaking her nose right open at the same time. There was blood all over the place. It was so nightmarish.

Discipline was more on the edge of child abuse. He mostly would use a leather belt lined with metal studs. He made those strikes count. One time Jeff and I got in trouble for stealing about a buck fifty from Ray's younger brother, so Ray decided the metal-studded belt wouldn't be enough. He used an extension cord instead. It left welts for weeks. Jeff and I finally had enough so we decided to run away for good. Helen and Bob had already left some time ago. Helen went to live with her cousins from her father's side, while Bobby drifted in and out of Juvenile Hall as a result of joining the Earth Angel's gang.

Jeff and I were both arrested for running away about a week or so later. We told the police with red crying faces about all of the abuse and how we wanted to go live with Blade, our dad. There were no police reports, no investigation by social services, we were returned to my mom and Ray. It wasn't long before Ray would continue with the abuse. Soon after our return, Ray's son knocked over a large barrel of aluminum cans he was collecting. He told me to clean it up, knowing full well his son had knocked it over. I asked him if it was his son who knocked it over. With that he attacked me, kicking me and beating me with his fists as though I were a grown man. Up to that point I don't think I had ever hated anyone. I never felt so much hate in my life. Any ounce of life left inside of me was killed on that day. I had nothing left. I had made up my mind to totally harden my heart as I walked away from the beating with tears streaming down my face, cries that would go unheard by my mom or Blade. I was going to prove to everyone I was hard-core and could care less about anyone or anything. As much as I felt like I hated Ray, becoming hard core seemed like the only alternative to gaining Ray's and my mother's respect.

  The gang members Helen and Bob hung around with treated me with respect. This made me feel like I mattered. They were nice to me and joked around with me. To them I seemed to be somebody. I began to dress and act like them. Whenever they came around I was right there, admiring and looking up to them, hoping for some recognition. I gave up the nice friends I had from school. I began stealing, drinking and taking drugs regularly. I started off with sniffing glue, and gasoline in a sock, or in a plastic baggy. I started smoking cigarettes daily. I remember one day when Doug, Jeff, and I had gone out and stole some tubes of rubber cement. After squeezing some out inside our baggies we started sniffing the fumes. Out of nowhere I realized this wasn't me. I asked myself why I was doing it. I was at a crossroad in my heart, looking for any excuse to return to the true me. Unfortunately, I told myself I had to do this if I wanted to be accepted. I continued sniffing on the fumes until I hallucinated. This hallucination was purely demonic. The sun had gone down when I was sitting out back on an old dirty couch in a dirty old shed next to the garage. I heard the most dark and demonic laugh I had ever heard in all my life. I looked down at my right hand to see a neon green ring glowing on my ring finger. I was trying desperately to remove it as the laugh grew stronger and the dark demonic presence grew thicker. I panicked and ran out of the shed only to hear a demonic voice say to me, "you belong to me now, and you'll never get away, aha, ha, ha, ha". I stood there, stunned, looking at the ring, until it disappeared with the hallucination. You'd think that would be enough to scare a 12-year-old out of heading down the wrong path. Everywhere things kept getting worse.

By this time we moved to a house on State Street, across the street from the rail road tracks, about two miles from the grain mills, where the mills filled the train cars with grain. My mom and Ray were selling drugs out of the house. They had two kids by that time. My drinking and drug use had increased as well. I became violent; beating on those I knew wouldn't fight back, or at least wouldn't have much of a chance to win. Jeff and I were constantly fighting.

The last glue sniffing hallucination I could remember was when my cousin Doug and I were under the house in a crawl space. We sat on the dirt floor where there was only about two to three feet of height to crawl through. We were sitting next to support beams on one side of us. On the other side were two large boards that crossed, forming an X. With Doug sitting next to me we began sniffing our glue until we hallucinated. All of a sudden the ground started moving backwards. I looked over at my cousin and he had turned into Satan.

Satan was laughing at me with that same demonic laugh as in the earlier hallucination. His finger pointed down to the ground, he said as he laughed, "You're going to hell with me and there's no escape, ha, ha, ha, ha...." I immediately went to get away and turned to the other side, but the crossbars blocked me in. In my mind I was stuck and literally on my way to hell with Satan himself as my host. I came out of the trip only to find Doug laughing at me. I was scared as scared could be.

My parents did a good job at preparing Bobby for the mob lifestyle. All throughout his teen years he was in and out of Juvenile Hall. He went to live with our dad Blade when he was thirteen-years old. Blade continued to be heavily involved in the Arian Brotherhood and running drugs for them. Bobby came back home after ripping Blade off for his drug stash and drug money. When Bob was about sixteen years old, he broke out of Juvenile Hall. He scaled a tall wall that was covered in barbed wire. As suspected by the police he came back to the neighborhood. My mom finally talked him into turning himself in, and for whatever reason they dropped the charges against him, and let him out. He told me horror stories about being locked up in Juvy, as it was called. The sad part about Juvenile Hall is even though it is a horrible place to go, you gain more respect on the streets for the more time you do. You are seen as being a hard-core gang member.

There were two main gangs that ruled our part of town. The Black Angels gang on the east side, and the

Earth Angel's on the south side of town. Both the Black Angels and the EA's were made up of older adults, mainly in the mid to late twenties and thirties. Each gang probably had about one hundred plus members. These men controlled the drug traffic in our part of town. They were responsible for various robberies and vandalism around town. They had families of their own. Most of them were in and out of prison. Some were members of the Mexican Mafia, otherwise known as the Eme. The EA's also had a junior gang in town. The Jr. EA's were a lot older than the members of the Junior Black Angels. Most of these guys were in their late teens and early twenties, whereas the Jr. Black Angels were mostly twelve to sixteen-year olds. A lot of the Jr. EA's had cars, primered low riders mostly. These guys were hard-core gang members, very close to graduating to the senior gang. The Jr. Black Angels didn't stand a chance against the Jr. EA's gang.

 After Bobby (a.k.a. Huero) got out of juvy, he came back home. He had been in the Jr. EA's for some time now. He was always in trouble. His gang friends hung around our house. In fact our house became the party place for the EA's. I felt I had proven myself ready to join the gang. I did not know what I was getting involved in. One of the gang members from the Earth Angel's they called Panther asked me if I wanted to join. Against my brothers wishes I said yes. Bobby knew it wasn't me, yet he didn't stop me. Panther told me to plan on attending next Fridays meeting for initiation. Before that meeting took place, on one particular day I went over to my girlfriend's house and as it turned out the President of the Jr. EA's was there visiting her older brother who himself was a member of the Senior Earth Angel's gang. He introduced himself as

Santos. He drove a 1969 Chevy Impala Lowrider. He sported a goat-tee mustache and presented himself as the coolest and toughest vato around. Santos asked who I was, and immediately knew about me because of Huero. Santos was in his mid twenties. He lived in the heart of Earth Angel territory and came from a long line of gang members. His home had several bullet holes in the wall from previous drive by shootings. His older brother was a wino who told everyone stories about the gang days in the 50's and 60's. Santos hung around with a small group of hard-core gang members. This core group made up the leadership of the Earth Angel's gang. Santos never came across as being hard-core or crazy. He spoke proper English, as well as Spanish; he was educated and had a regular job. He was charismatic in that he was nice to everyone. You would never have guessed he personally gave the orders to recruit young teens into the gang life, as well as giving the orders to vandalize, commit robbery, and to murder rival gang members and even innocent citizens who somehow became ensnared in the trappings of gang life.

    Friday had approached. The meeting was held early in the evening at the local elementary school. Most of the gang members had already been drinking, including myself. There were about thirty guys at the meeting. I was too buzzed to notice they were all at least five to ten years older than I was and twice as big. The time came for the gang to decide on an initiation. This time it would be the gauntlet, or liñe. To join the gang you had to prove you were tough, could give blows, and take them at the same time. If not, they would beat you till you couldn't walk anymore. There was no turning back now; I already said I would join the gang. I didn't want to change my mind. What else was there?

The gang broke off into two groups. The first fifteen members formed a line, shoulder to shoulder. The next fifteen members formed a line opposite the first group, shoulder to shoulder. Both lines of gang members were facing each other. The object was to get through the line fighting your way through all thirty guys. The first to go through was a big guy they nicknamed Batman. Batman was a football player from the local High School. When they gave him the signal he covered his face and ran through the line of gang members as though he was carrying a football. I think the gang members were a little upset because he made it through so easily. Fortunately Santos, the Prez, told all the members to take it easy on me because of my age and size. Unfortunately, my brother Huero told me to be tough and fight my way through before it was my turn to go. I got the signal and went in slugging the first few guys. I heard, "Oh, this kid thinks he's tough". They all jumped on me. I was still punching, only now with my eyes closed, I felt nothing but blows all over my upper body. Finally, one of the older gang members took a punk shot and hit me square in the nose. The gang broke loose and I came out with teary eyes from the broken nose and all the pride in the world as the gang members were excitedly welcoming me into the gang. I was quickly accepted by most of the main members, though they were not supposed to have let me in because of my age. One day I was wearing my gang sweater in the hood when a Senior EA saw me for the first time. He asked me how old I was. I lied and said I was fifteen-years old. I was only thirteen.

My official nickname would be Sleepy. Huero

had been in the gang for some time. My sister Helen, a.k.a. Smiley, was the vice-president of the girl's version of the Earth Angel's, called the Lady EA's. These girls weren't there to wait on the guys. They were actual gang members who could hold their own. A lot of them were unwed-mothers and some were dealing drugs on their own, which is really sad. I heard my sister tell me story after story of the gang riots and shootouts the Lady EA's would have with other female gangs from other towns, as well as about cruise nights in Los Angeles on the Sunset Strip. She said there were a lot of shootings and murders that took place.

    The Jr. EA's were what law officials would classify as an organized gang. That is one step below organized crime, the Mafia. I can recall when a position in the gang's leadership for the position of treasurer became available. We had a meeting and Santos told anyone interested to stand up. I stood up with about four other guys. We all looked at each other and then back at Santos, waiting for the vote. Santos told us all to fight it out; last one standing had the position. It was too late to sit down now. Fortunately he was joking. His younger brother was voted as treasurer. Chato, the Vice President of the EA's would fill in for Santos when he was away and would otherwise assist him. The Sergeant of Arms was responsible for taking care of and obtaining weapons. These weapons were anything from switchblade knives to handguns; semi-automatic rifles, and sawed off shotguns.

    Some of the gang members had notorious reputations. There was Rico and his younger brother Santana. Rico was well over six feet tall and well built. If any one of our guys needed a beating, he'd be one of the first picks to carry out the punishment. No one outside of the gang was safe with him. He had robbed an Ice Cream Truck twice by gunpoint. During one meeting, a member of the gang was on trial for running away from a riot, leaving his fellow gang members to fight on their own. A free-for-all was to be the punishment. Rico and two other gang members openly beat the guy with their bare fists; all the while the police were parked nearby, observing the whole thing. I can recall another time when the EA's were gearing up for a riot with the Black Angels in our own territory. I was in the same car as Rico. I watched as we came to a screeching halt in front of a police car. Two Policemen were out of their car motioning for us to stop. When Rico and a couple of the other guys quickly got out of the car I was surprised to see the cops quickly jump back into their patrol car. They got one good look at Rico and decided they would monitor the situation from inside of their patrol car. The Black Angels never showed.

  Then there was Flaco and his older brother Mad Dog. These two brothers defined what a hard core gang member was all about. Flaco was a short muscular guy who could pack a good punch. Mad Dog was about Santos' age. He was buff and was a good boxer. They grew up in the house right on the corner where as I had mentioned earlier a mother had lost her baby while crossing the street when I was a little kid. They lived with both of their parents; however, their dad was an alcoholic. My sister would become close to this family in the coming years and would marry Mad Dog in part because of my mothers prodding. There was a lot of talk about doing drive-by shootings. How they would see guys going down after being shot. The gangsters would come to the meetings with cases of beer they had stolen from the local liqueur store.

It wasn't long before I hooked up with a partner in crime named Gato. I went to Junior High with his younger sister. His family lived nearby mine, about five miles away from our gang's hangout. When we moved even farther away, we came to find out his family moved to the same neighborhood about the same time as ours. There were a few times when my parents took the family out to the park or to the amusement park and oddly enough we would run into Gato's family at the same event. So after joining the gang Gato and I became friends. From getting loaded, stealing cars, robbing houses, to cruising together in his El Camino with the ladies, Gato and I hung out.

Gato and I decided to pay a visit late one Friday night to some old friends named Rod and Steve who were having a party to kick off their new neighborhood gang. They were calling it the Red Devils. I knew Rod and Steve from elementary school. We played kick ball and baseball together. Steve was my age and his brother was the same age as my older brother. They were racially mixed, yet looked more White than Mexican. I think Steven was tougher than Rod, which is why they had a hard time being accepted by the established neighborhood gangs. They had each tried to join a gang in our neighborhood, yet for different reasons were refused membership.

The Black Angel's and the EA's knew all about their attempts to start their own gang. There was a lot of talk in the hood. None of it was positive. I knew eventually one of the organized gangs in our neighborhood would come down hard on them to keep the gang from starting. I knew at least one of these guys would end up dead as a result. This is the reason I wanted to show up to the party. To warn them, and let them know it was a very bad idea. Gato only wanted to go to put the leader of the Red Devils in check and to pick up on his girl friend in front of his face. At the party Gato kept mad dogging one of the members and almost got into it with Rod, Prez of the Red Devils. Rod backed down. We left the party early. On the way back to Gatos house we heard several gunshots coming from the direction of the party. The Earth Angel's had secretly planned to do a drive by shooting at the Red Devils party that night to send a message. The house was riddled with bullets as Rod, Steve and the rest of them all jumped for the floor. A bullet barely missed Rod. No one was injured. The gang disbanded and was never heard of again.

     Several years later I would hear of the shocking death of Steven. He was found stabbed to death in Rod's abandoned van. It turned out he and his older brother Rod had been smoking LSD together, which is a hallucinogenic drug. Rod began to hallucinate. During his hallucination he took his buck knife and repeatedly stabbed Steven to death.

     On another occasion Gato and I decided to walk around town late at night looking for unlocked cars. After which we would take whatever we could find. We found an older car that was unlocked and we were able to start it without a key. Our adrenaline was pumping fast. Gato took the wheel and off we went. We weren't the smartest criminals, just a couple of punk kids trying to use their free time creatively. I suppose we should have stolen a newer model car. We didn't notice until much later one of the headlights was pointing to the stars. The cop waiting for speeding cars noticed it too. Seconds later the dreaded flashing blue and red lights were shining in the review mirror. His intent was to give us a fix-it ticket. Gatos story about test-driving our uncle's car to help him fix it at midnight worked for a while. That is until the call came in to the police station about a missing car with a headlight pointing toward the sky. I felt bad for lying to the police officer. He had given me the benefit of the doubt. We were off to juvenile hall. Being a passenger in the car and a first time offender I was out in three days. Gato was convicted for grand theft auto and got over a year of time.

 Shortly after his release Gato nearly lost his life after being jumped by some gang members from another town. Gato was unarmed. They had tire irons they used to repeatedly beat him over the head until he lay unconscious. His skull was in pieces. His girlfriend rushed him to the hospital. After several surgeries they were able to save his life. He was away from the gang meetings for a long time while he healed from his wounds.

 The gang members who jumped him went to prison for the crime. They were locked up with one of the Sr. Earth Angel's. When you're locked up in jail you have no choice but to get along with gang members from other towns in your area, no matter what has happened in your hood. If you don't get along, you leave yourself open to being killed by gang members from other ethnic groups, such as the white mob, or black gangs. So instead of claiming say, East Los Angeles, in prison you would claim Southern California. Therefore, the Earth Angel gang member could do nothing to the gang members who jumped Gato. There was a truce.

 The gang members who jumped Gato took advantage of the truce and said Gato had ratted on them and that is why they were locked up. The last thing you want in the ghetto is to be called a snitch. As soon as Gato was well enough to be out and about, his own gang turned on him. Gato was pumping gas one day as an EA gang member came up to him, called him a rat, and then started beating on him. The sad part is they didn't even ask Gato whether or not it was true. They took the other guys word for it. It ended up Gato was dropped from the gang.

After about a year I was doing heavy drugs, and regularly dropping acid. I smoked LSD and PCP, and hung around with a heroin dealer in High School. I never tried heroin. The needle thing made it unattractive to me. I even tried different types of pills I got from my sister Helen. I was feeling like I had arrived somewhere special. I had respect. Getting a girl friend was easy. And most of all I was accepted. This longing I had always felt in the center of my chest, like some kind of emptiness or void in my heart, felt like it had finally been filled. I felt like I was one of the coolest gangsters when cruising in Santos' '69 Chevy Impala with the oldie's music blaring. I was looking forward to the day when I could go on a drive by shooting with the gang. I was feared in high school by most of the other gangsters. It was mostly out of respect for my gang. I was the only Jr. EA at my school. All the others were Crips, Bloods, and Jr Black Angels.

My freshman year in High School was a waste. All I did was smoke dope on my way to school; ditch most all my classes and cause trouble with the teachers and students. I had no intention of learning, my only purpose for going to school was to make connections and meet girls. After having gone to my math class for about the third time out of about 30 sessions, I walked up to the teacher seconds after the tardy bell rang to see what he'd say. He was about to take roll. He asked, "Who are you?" I was surprised he didn't remember me. I thought I stuck out pretty good with my baggy pants, shined shoes, slicked back hair, and dark shades. So I thought I'd have a little fun. I noticed a neighbor of mine was absent, so I responded, "why, I'm Ruben Rivera". "You're not Ruben Rivera", he shouted back. I looked behind me to see all the students laughing. So I looked on the seating chart and gave him my real name, "Ron..." pretending like I couldn't pronounce my Swedish last name. Boy was he mad. No matter how hard I tried I couldn't convince him I was who I said I was. The class kept on laughing. The joke was on me though. It turned out this teacher was the Superintendent of the Math Department for the School District. Not too long after I was caught in the hallway with a group of gang associates that got in trouble for beating a kid who happened to be walking by. I overheard my counselor telling the Principal of the school word for word she hated me. She wanted me expelled from the district. She got her way. When I overheard what she said it hit me how terrible I'd become. So far away from the person I was in my childhood and the person I had hopes of becoming in the future.

  It didn't take long before I would begin to see why my brother Huero had originally told me not to join the gang. The gang got together to go to a party. One of the gang members had rented out a public hall for the party. There must have been two or three kegs of beer. I thought I was being cool by drinking one beer after another. It didn't take long for the alcohol to catch up with me. Fighting broke out in the parking lot so we all went out to see what was going on. There were two or three different gangs represented that night. Not a good combination. An older man was trying to break up the fight when one of the Black Angels took his switchblade and cut the guys face open. Then Paul's younger brother Bandit, who had joined the Jr. Black Angels, jokingly called me a Lady EA. I laughed and called him a Black Angel Lady. He laughed and we did a gangster's handshake. I didn't realize it but Flaco from the Jr. EA's was standing right behind me. He didn't like what Bandit said to me, not realizing I had stood my ground. He confronted Bandit and without another word the two of them were in a fight. A Black Angel in his late twenties was chasing a Jr. EA around the parking lot, saying the guy stared at him the wrong way. It was nothing short of chaotic. I was left secretly wishing I had listened to my older brother about not joining the gang.

    I wasted school and spent my summers working for the government sponsored programs. I worked at the Air National Guard as a custodian trainee. I became a friend at work with this kid named Joe who had recently moved to California from Chicago. He was a nice guy. He hung around one of the Jr. EA gang members named Arnold. He told me he wanted to join our gang. I told him in all honesty not to. Being a walking target along with all of the drugs and violence was not all it seemed. To his regret he didn't listen. He joined in the same way I had. About a year later our gang had a riot with the Jr. Black Angels involving gunshots. One of the Jr. Black Angels was shot in the head and killed. They blamed Joe and put a contract out on his life. He had to move back to Chicago. It turned out it was my brother Huero who killed the kid, not Joe.

    One of the guys Joe and I worked with was from Chino, a nearby town. Their gang was called the Sinners.

This guy was in his early twenties. He now lived in our part of town and said he no longer was a Sinner gangster. He told me he could get some grenades for our gangs use. I never had a chance to take him up on that. Even though he was no longer with the Sinners, he had done some things to some gangsters from our part of town; as a result someone had it in for him. One day after work he pulled up to his house, not knowing a gang member was waiting for him with a double barreled sawed off shotgun. When my friend pulled up to his house, the gang member walked up to his car window, and shot both of the barrels at point blank range into his face. His head was gone. It was payback time - big time.

During this time my brother Bobby was busy getting in trouble with the EA's gang. He did a lot of things to get other gangs upset. At one time the Senior Black Angels did a drive by shooting at my house with a 30/30 rifle, leaving a couple of large bullet holes in the wall. Fortunately, no one was home. Santana, Ricos younger brother, committed suicide when he took the same type of gun and stuck it in his mouth, pulling the trigger. Everyone blamed his girlfriend for his suicide. She was probably the only good thing he had in this life. I would imagine he felt the same thing all of us felt: destitute with feelings of emptiness and despair over a life going nowhere fast. Worrying about your number being up, and feeling guilty as can be for all the hurt you've caused others, yet wanting nothing more than for both of your parent's involvement and support, yet getting nothing more than abandonment, along with the false sense of purpose that comes along with being in a gang. The emptiness and loneliness inside all of us was as vast and as deep as a Grand Canyon.

RIOT

It was a cool fall day, in the middle of September 1980, the skies were mostly gray and the cool crisp winds were blowing pretty steadily bringing my senses to life. Nothing, however, could prepare me for what was to take place on this particular Friday. The saying, "you reap what you sow" would take on a whole new meaning for the Earth Angel's on this particular day.

The gang was not meeting at our usual hang out that evening so I made plans during the day with a couple of non-gang member friends from school, named Snoop and Freddie. I was in the ninth grade and attending one of the oldest High Schools in the Inland Empire. My grandma attended Chaffey High School when she was a teen. The school looked more like an old Ivy League College with its old buildings than a High School. Most of the gang types attending Chaffey High were members of the Black Angels, the Bloods, or the Crips territory. Snoops older brothers were long time members of the Black Angels. I had met Snoops older brother during the summer; he was a hard-core gangster, yet he was nice to the younger teens like me. When I met Snoop in High School we hit it off and became friends. Freddie was Snoops friend. I didn't know him yet I figured if he was all right with Snoop, then he was all right with me. I figured we would meet around five o'clock in the evening at my place, pick up some wine, and then head on over to my friend Betty's house to score some weed. Betty lived about a mile from Snoop's house. She lived in a shack with her three sisters and her single mom. She never knew her father, only the

many boy friends her mom would party with at her home.
That same evening several of the Earth Angel's had planned on going to a party in the nearby town of Pomona, which is in Los Angles County. My brother Huero along with my brother-in-law Mad Dog, and his younger brother Flaco were planning to go along. The leadership of the gang would be there as well, to include Chato, the President of the gang.

The most notorious gang in Pomona is called the 12th Street Sharks. No gang I know of got along with this gang. These gang members were hard-core, cold-blooded killers. They would cruise into other gang territory on a regular basis, if you happened to be walking alone or in a small group, whether or not you were related to someone from Shark territory, they would kill you. And kill they did. I heard a lot of horror stories about this gang. How they jumped a guy right in front of a Liquor store with tire irons until his head was gone. One of the guys in our gang was riding his bike home one evening, when the Sharks spotted him, without warning and without fear of being seen by any bystanders, they ran him over with their car, leaving him for dead. I mention this gang because the EA's went to Pomona to party with the girls from the 12th Street Sharks gang. As tough as most of the guys were from the EA's gang this was not a smart move, gutsy, but not at all smart.

Early that evening I met Snoop and Freddie as planned. Meanwhile, the EA's met the 12th Street girls at an abandoned parking lot in Pomona. Everything was going pretty smooth for the EA's until word got out to the gang members from the 12th Street Sharks; they showed up ready for a riot. The fighting started right away. Our gang was unprepared. No guns, knives, or weapons, just their fists. The Sharks didn't have any guns, but managed to bring some stabbing instruments such as ice picks. The fist fighting went on for some time. The EA's fought as long as they could, until there were more Sharks than they could handle. The Sharks brought out their weapons. Mad Dog and Huero fought several gang members off. Mad Dog got in-between his brother Flaco and a Shark gang member as the Shark swung with an ice pick. As Mad Dog fought off this gang member he yelled to his brother to run, and run he did as Mad Dog stayed behind so the others could escape. Mad Dog ended up stabbed two or three times in the chest with the ice pick. He kept fighting as though nothing had happened, until he was able to get away himself. Needless to say, Mad Dog was one of the toughest vatos in our gang. Later that evening Mad Dog came to my house so Helen could take him to the hospital. It was unreal. Mad Dog was just standing there with open holes in his chest, as though nothing had happened at all. My sister Helen was freaked. He was fortunate the ice pick didn't pierce any vital organs or veins. He made it through alive. Little did I know the worst part of the evening was yet to come.

    After the riot with the EA's, the 12th Street Sharks called an emergency meeting with all of their available gang members. They met at their usual hang out, a park on 12th street, where during the day innocent children play ball and all sorts of games. The plan was to send three of their craziest, most violent gang members to our hang out. They were to capture one of our gang members and kill him. Thereafter, they were to take his bloodied gang shirt so they could bring it back to prove they had killed one of us. Revenge and murder was the plan.

After Mad Dog and Helen left to the hospital, Snoop, Freddie, and I decided to put our change together and buy a couple of bottles of cheap liquor and then head on over to my friend Betty's house. I grabbed my gang sweater and off we went. Kim's Market was the neighborhood store in my area and was owned by an Asian couple. This was one of my hangouts, and is where the neighborhood kids bought cigarettes and liquor. We bought a pack of smokes and a bottle of Midnight, a cheap wine. Betty and her sisters went cruising before we arrived. We knew they'd be back soon so we waited. By the time the sun had set the liquor was gone. Betty and her sisters returned upset. It turned out they had gone cruising down by the abandoned parking lot in Pomona. They were unaware of the riot that had taken place a short time before they cruised through the area. Some of the 12th Street Sharks were still there. When they spotted Betty's car they bottled it with beer bottles. I was already upset about the attack on the Earth Angel's, and now this. With the cheap wine in full effect, Snoop and I decided the three of us would head out to Pomona to somehow get back at the 12th Street Sharks.

Around midnight a friend of mine named Tony stopped by in an old car with a friend of his. Tony was Psycho's cousin. He was an older teen and was more Huero and Helen's friend than mine. He was fast becoming the neighborhood wino. After telling Tony all about the 12th Street Sharks he and the driver decided to take us down to the abandoned parking lot in Pomona. Tony and his friend were passed being drunk. Tony couldn't stand straight and started to become more of a problem to the group. His friend was even drunker than he was so Tony was the one who drove the car. I suppose that was to make it safer. Snoop and I decided to ditch Tony, so when he got out to take care of his business I hopped in the front seat and drove away. Tony stood there in the alleyway with his mouth dropped open as we drove away. His friend didn't seem to mind too much being he was passed out on the passenger side of the front seat. We were on our way to Pomona down a dark and narrow street named State Street. State Street ran parallel to the Rail Road tracks. On one side of the tracks were mostly grain mills used to fill the train cars with tons of grain and feed. On the other side of the road, opposite of the tracks, were miles of abandoned strawberry fields and empty grain vats.

    By this time it was about one in the morning. I was pretty drunk myself. Driving the old bomb of a car down State Street proved to be a real challenge. I was doing everything I could not to sideswipe the fence to the right of me that bordered the water ditch and the road. The alcohol made it hard, yet to make matters worse, this was my first time behind the wheel of a car. I noticed two bright headlights following me very closely. I kept looking back between the fence and the headlights, the fence and the headlights, trying my best not to crash. Then suddenly, as I had feared, the red and blue lights started flashing in my rear-view mirror. It had been a police car following me. I turned right onto the next available street, practically driving into the opposite side of traffic. As I was stopping I tried to awake the drunken man in the seat next to me. He wouldn't budge. To wake him I slammed on the breaks, finally coming to a complete stop. I told him we had been pulled over by the cops.

The Officer asked him if he knew he had a fourteen-year-old driving his car. He was over apologizing, saying he didn't know I was so young. The Officer asked Snoop, Freddie, and me why we were out driving around at one in the morning. I didn't have an answer. The police had the main switch board call my parents to come and pick us up. As was typical of my mom and her boyfriend, having been abandoned as a child, she once again left me out in the cold. She told the police to have us walk home. After getting off his band radio, the cop told the three of us to start walking home. By the time I was pulled over, I had driven to the next city, about five miles from my house. So, at about one thirty on a Saturday morning, pitch black at night, the three of us young teens started walking back home.

While Snoop, Freddie, and I were walking we were talking about what a bad night it had been, unaware of the danger that was coming from behind. As we were walking down State Street, unknown to the three of us the 12th Street Sharks were on their way to carry out their murderous plans for revenge against the Earth Angel's. The quickest way for them to get to the EA territory from Pomona was to go down State Street.

I remember feeling like we were walking in slow motion, as though time had stopped for the moment. That's when we noticed the round headlights coming from behind us. We moved over to the side of the road, next to an abandoned strawberry field, only blocks away from Snoops house. On the other side of the street you could see the black silhouettes of the train cars and the grain mills. It was totally silent, as though the oncoming car had no running engine at all. The car pulled over to the side, right in front of Snoop and Freddie. It was a gold toned 1969 Chevy Impala low rider, with a crack in the windshield.

Snoop and Freddie talked to them for what seemed to be forever, and then I heard a shout from inside of the Low Rider car, "what gang are you from?" I knew they were talking to me and that Snoop and Freddie had backed down from representing the side of town they claimed. Snoop and Freddie backed away knowing there was no way I would back down, even if it meant death. "Earth Angel's rule", I responded back. Immediately the gang member in the front seat threw his beer bottle at me, hitting me in the face. The bottle cut my upper lip open just beneath my nose, my face went numb.

The 12th Street Sharks who had fought with my gang earlier that evening were inside the Low Rider; they found their target. "He's got a gun!," Snoop shouted. I turned and started running away from the car in the direction of the field. Before I could take three steps, "BLAM, BLAM," gunshots were fired, shattering the silence. I shrieked in pain as two searing hot bullets went into my back at point blank range, one bullet ricocheting inside my intestines, tearing them to shreds. I grabbed my back where the bullets entered, I was nearly lifted off of the ground each time I was hit by a bullet, I was in total shock and dismay, as my worst fears became reality. Snoop and Freddie dropped to the ground to avoid being shot. I jumped down as well hoping the shooting would stop, only to look behind me as one of the gang members got out of the car with a knife, coming straight for me; the nightmare grew worse. I got up and started running into the dark field. My heart was pounding a mile a minute, and my entire being filled with horror, as I heard more gunshots ring out, "BLAM, BLAM, BLAM". Two more screaming bullets pierced my back, one of the bullets lodged in my rib on the right side of my chest, above my stomach. My mind went completely numb, I couldn't feel my body, all I could feel were my feet running beneath me. I thought of my mom as I was running for my life, I called out to her in horror, yet I was alone as always, with no protection, her face immediately faded from my mind.

In shock I kept on running into the field with four bullet holes in my back, jumping over mounds of dirt and grassy weeds illuminated by the light of the full moon. When your body is in shock, you don't stop to wonder whether or not it is possible for your body to run. You run, and I ran as fast as I possibly could. Snoop and Freddie caught up to me as I reached a chain link fence at the end of the field. They hopped over it like nothing. As I reached the top I froze in terror, yelling for Snoop and Freddie to help me, as they disappeared into the darkness. I couldn't run anymore. My body wouldn't let me. My homeboys left me to die. I knew my attacker was seconds behind me with his razor sharp knife clenched tight in his fist. The gang member chasing me with the knife caught up to me and began stabbing me in my left leg. This wasn't a problem for him as all three of the gang members were strung out on powerful drugs called LSD.

My muscles tightened and I went completely stiff and jolted up with shock as I felt the ice-cold blade pierce the back of my leg. I let go of the fence and landed on my head, which knocked me out cold, so I didn't feel it while the gang member repeatedly stabbed me over fifteen times all over both my arms, my back, as well as on my chest and on my side. The stab wound to my side was the most lethal because my attacker punctured my right lung with the blade of his knife. I finally regained consciousness while he was kicking me with his steel-toed shoes in my face and on my head. He was trying to take off my gang sweater, which had the name and logo of the Earth Angel's. All I could see was a haze and darkness. I could not feel the many wounds on my body, I could not feel the blunt kicks to my head and face. I was half dead and my body was in total shock. When I realized the adult gang member was after my sweater, I raised my arms and let go of it fully realizing, although too late, it was not worth dying for. He had what he came for, a bloodied sweater of a brutally murdered Earth Angel gang member. All that was left to do was make for certain I was dead.

    My attacker stood over me with the bloodied knife. I did not want to look at his face, all I could do was just helplessly lie there and live through this nightmare, as I hear the gunman running in our direction. The gunman shouted, "Where is he?" "Over here, homes", the man with the knife responded, leaving me alone with the gunman. He was sent to make sure I was dead, and he was determined to finish me off with a single gunshot to the head.

    I lay there, my body numbed from the trauma and shock of this nightmarish violence, as the ground soaked up my blood. I finally looked up to see the gunman stand there like a marksman holding his pistol in both of his hands. His arms stretched out in front of him, making his aim right at my forehead. I could feel the bullet breaking through my skull and into my brain before he pulled the trigger. My imagination played out the terror of what I was witnessing, a cold harsh realization moments before one's death. I knew that once he pulled the trigger, this would be the final blow; there would be no surviving this shot, I was at the end of the line for good.

 I didn't want this to be the last thing I would see in my life; I didn't want to see the blast of fire come out of the barrel of the gun. This man was a cold-blooded mass murderer that could look a child in the eyes as he pulls the trigger. I covered my eyes with my bloodied arm, and did the sign of the Cross. It was my last chance at hope. I knew deep down that after the gun went off I would be dead, and what scared me the most is not knowing where I stood with God. I needed to make my peace with God, there was nowhere else to turn. The gun didn't go off so I immediately moved my arm down enough to see my attacker, only to witness something touch the most inner part of this gunman's darkened soul. As I looked I saw him throw his head back, as he said in amazement, "woe". He lowered his gun just a bit and asked me, "Do you believe in God?" I moved my arm out of the way, with my bloodied face mixed with tears, I answered, "yes, I do believe in God." The gang member put his gun down and said, "Oh well, you're going to die anyhow, 12th Street Sharks". With that he left.

 My attackers are gone, Snoop and Freddie are gone, and my body riddled with bullet holes and multiple stab wounds, completely bloodied all over. I am alone and left for dead. Everyone I trusted abandoned me to die – including my mom – when she told the police to have her fourteen-year old son walk home at one in the morning. I looked out to the stars. The night was dead silent. I could hear myself breathing long deep breaths, as though that were the only sound in the Universe; my heart beating heavy within me. I was overcome with the stark reality of my life. All I had been living for was worth nothing at all, and in the end NOT WORTH DYING FOR. It was all I had, all I knew. It wasn't even worth living for. I lost the will to go on. All I had left within was despair and despondency; as a result I decided I didn't want to survive my wounds. I wanted to die. I was destitute; all hope was gone. I held my breath to quicken my death; to make sure I would die, as tears flowed from my eyes down my cheeks onto the blood soiled dirt.

    At that very moment, in my darkest hour, Jesus Christ broke through the darkness and silence as He spoke life to my heart and mind, changing my deep despair and hopelessness into peace and hope as Jesus spoke to my heart, I heard it so unmistakably clear, saying, "Ron, there is a reason to live. You will know I Am the reason". At that instant God touched my heart and the inner pain and hopelessness vanished, the sky seemed to light up. The stars shone brighter than ever before, as though blinders had been taken off of my eyes. What my physical eyes could not see, my soul could hear loud and clear. I was not alone in that cold dark field after all. It was the presence of Jesus Christ. God entered my nightmare to rescue me, giving me the motivation to survive my wounds, and the courage to once again have hopes and dreams for the future. Miracles started to happen in an abandoned strawberry field in the mean streets of Southern California.

    I started gasping for air, not because I was out of breath, or because my lung was collapsing, yet because I now had something worth living for. I knew in my heart as the Lord Jesus had said, I would soon know what the true meaning for living is. I knew in my heart it has everything to do with Jesus Christ. Miracles started to happen right then and there. The hand of God was in control over this fourteen-year olds life. When God is in control – nothing is impossible.

Within seconds I heard a rustling in the bushes behind the fence. I called out to see who was there. It was Snoops older brother Johnny. He came up to me and pushed on my shoulder, asking me if I'd been shot, as my body shook each time he pressed down. He called to Snoop and Freddie telling them to run and call the police. After waiting with me for a couple of minutes he said he would run back to get Snoop and Freddie. He left me alone. Soon afterward I saw the police cars passing by the field with their searchlights on. I pulled together all the energy I possibly could. I couldn't die now. I pulled myself up off the blood-soiled dirt with all the physical strength I had left, I wanted to run back to the road, yet my feet would not move. I stood there waving my hand in the air, trying to flag down the passing police car, yet he did not see me, and kept going. I could feel the blood gushing out of my leg so fast that my blood-soaked pants lifted off of my leg. With that I literally fell over and landed on my back with a thud. Just then Snoop came back with his brother Johnny. Johnny sent the two to the street to flag down the police.

Immediately afterward I could see a police car driving through the field straight for us. My heart was glad; I knew I'd be saved. Within a minute the ambulance was there. The emergency team stripped me of my blood-drenched clothing. By this time I was shivering cold at the brink of death. The lead emergency medical tech said

I was in too bad of shape to work on there. They put me on the gurney, put the various I.V. needles in my arms, along with the oxygen mask, and drove as fast as they possibly could to the local hospital, with the sirens and lights blaring. I felt sure that just as Christ spoke to my heart that I would be all right. I knew it was okay to rest now. I fell unconscious.

The next time I gained consciousness I was laying in the emergency ward at the Ontario Community Hospital. My mom was standing at my side. My brother Bobby and sister Helen came up to me when they realized I had awakened. I could see and hear monitors beeping and blipping, tubes hooked up to my body. Bobby and Helen asked me who had done this to me so I told them it was the 12th Street Sharks. The cops saw us talking and immediately rushed over to me and started drilling me with questions. They asked me who had done this, I wouldn't tell them. I wanted to tell them so badly, yet my past experiences with the police would not allow me to trust them when I should have. I also remembered the rule of the streets, never ever rat on anyone. Your "homies" will take care of it for you. Otherwise, your own "homies" will turn on you. So I told the police I didn't know who my attackers were. Finally the doctors told the police to leave me alone.

I was still dying because the Emergency Doctor did not feel he had the needed level of expertise to treat the severity of my wounds. As a result he was going to let me die. It was at that precise moment that my family Doctor passed by and saw my mom standing over me. He asked her, "Marie, what are you doing here"? She pointed to me and without any hesitation he gave the order, "take him to the operating room, STAT!" It so happened my family doctor, who had treated me for asthma since I was seven-years old, had stopped by the hospital to check on a patient of his on the way home from a late engagement. Jesus Christ in His perfect timing created a miracle and came through to keep His promise to show me He truly is the reason worth living for.

The last thing I remembered before going under sedation was being wheeled into the operating room. The operation took over eight hours. The bullets did severe damage to my digestive system. My Doctor had to open my abdomen during the surgery and remove two and a half feet of my intestines where the bullets had ricocheted inside of my body. Two of the bullets were found and removed. Another was lodged in one of my ribs. Some of the knife wounds were closed during the surgery using surgical staples, however, on most of the stab wounds the Doctor simply bandaged them up. I had lost most of my blood supply. On top of all that, because the knife punctured my right lung, my right lung collapsed. I received several blood transfusions. I was told my head had swollen to the size of a basketball from the blunt kicks to my face. My parents were told the chances of my survival were slim to none, that I most likely would not live to see another day. My young body had been through too much. I had lost too much blood, along with having a collapsed right lung to deal with. It would be an uphill climb, with all of the odds stacked against me.

After attacking me the three 12th Street Shark gang members returned to their hang out where their gang was waiting in anticipation for their "victorious" return. The 1969 Chevy Impala with a cracked windshield pulled up and out came the three-gang members with their prize. My bloodied gang sweater, riddled with bullet holes and slashes from the razor sharp blade of the knife. They worked themselves into a frenzy, and started dancing and shouting around a bonfire; like warriors celebrating a kill. Next they set the sweater on fire and shouted in the darkness as it burned to ashes.

I learned first hand what took place that night from a man who was there with the 12th Street Sharks gang as they burned my sweater. He wasn't a part of the gang. He had an outreach to this particular gang, occasionally going there, putting his life in danger trying to reach some of these hard-core gang members. He was a Christian man who went by Mr. Lopez. It just so happened that Mr. Lopez was also the Assistant Principal of the Junior High School I attended in the seventh and eighth grades. He knew me well. He was at the Shark Gang's hang out that night and witnessed the whole thing. He had no idea at the time that the bloodied sweater belonged to one of his former students.

Meanwhile, back at the hospital, my family was told by my Doctor that it would be best if everyone visited me one last time because I would die soon. They were allowed to visit me two at a time. That is when I remember waking up for the first time after the operation in the isolation room of the Intensive Care Unit, when I sensed that someone very dear to me was at my side, and with that I woke up to see my Aunt Barbara and my Aunt Ricky crying at my side. For a moment I once again felt like a young child that would spend the night over at their homes so long ago. Neither of them was involved in gangs and they stayed away from trouble. I couldn't talk or much less communicate. I put my swollen-bandaged hand on my Aunt Barbara's arm and told her it was going to be okay. Moments later I was unconscious once again.

  The next time I awoke I remember once again having this sense of someone's presence in the room. I must have used every ounce of energy in my body to wake up. I was still heavily sedated and in the isolation room of the ICU. I regained consciousness with a major gasp for air. Just then, for the first time in many years, I saw my dad Blade walking away with tears in his eyes. I called out to him. It had been too long. All he could do was hold my hand until I fell unconscious once again. He was a hard man; his tears said everything he could not put into words.

  My body was heavily sedated and still in shock. I kept going in and out of consciousness. I had tubes going directly into my stomach through my stomach wall, and tubes going in through my nose to the inside of my stomach to drain out all of the fluids. My digestive system had completely shut down.

  My brother and sister didn't think I would make it. At one point my brother Bobby was holding my hand. He and Helen told me to squeeze his hand if I could hear them. Instead of squeezing his hand my arm dropped dead onto the bed. They freaked out thinking I had died. Sometime later on Bob told me that I was talking to him about what to do if I died, to make sure he looked after mom, to make sure she was taken care of. I don't remember talking to him at all, yet I know there had always been a special place in my heart for my mom, despite the years of neglect.

  After that, I was in a coma for about a week in the Isolation Unit of Intensive Care. After some time passed, I started to wake up regularly. I began looking at the bandages, wondering what the wounds must have looked like. I ran the tips of my fingers up and down my stomach, feeling the thick surgical staples that held my abdomen shut. I counted my wounds, four bullet holes in my back; the bullets narrowly missing my spinal cord. Seventeen puncture wounds from the blade of the knife. Not counting the wounds from the operation. Some of the knife wounds were wider than others, depending on how deep the knife penetrated my body. There were knife wounds on my leg, all over my back, on my chest, and on my side. There was even one on my right forearm. The tubes in my nose bothered me so I decided it would be a good idea to pull them out. So I did, just as the Intensive Care Nurse was walking by my isolation unit. She was excited I had come around, but a bit worried about what I did. She put the tubes back in. That was no fun. There was still trouble with my right lung so my Doctor ordered a tube to be placed inside my right lung through my chest wall. The Respiratory Doctor came in and inserted the tube right through the puncture wound made by the knife. I was already sedated, yet I was still awake. It was a hard procedure to endure.

  The Doctors said I had a very strong will to live. Most people I know of who had been shot once, or at most twice in the same area I had been shot had died, usually instantly. God had a plan for my life. This new found hope excited me, filling my whole being with the hope I needed to go on. Within two weeks I was out of Intensive Care and in a regular hospital unit. My friends came by to visit me. It took a few days thereafter to be able to walk. My legs were quite weak from the knife wounds as well as from having been inactive for some time. By the third week I was home. I wasn't fully functional; I slept quite a bit, but soon would recover. The one thing the 12th Street Sharks didn't realize when they had their victory dance is God Almighty had snatched the victory out of their hands; this time the victory belonged to God.

After going through this traumatizing attack I decided I would no longer go to the gang meetings. I realized the gang life wasn't worth dying for, much less living for. I wanted to turn my life over to God. I was glad to see my childhood friends and family when they visited me in the hospital and at home after my release. Now I had a reason to live, and a bright future that still needed to be discovered. The nightmare seemed to be over, it was safe to dream of a future once again, however, there were still many obstacles that lay ahead, obstacles that usually prove to be too difficult for most people to make it out of the street life.

R.K. Jensen

PROMISE KEPT

The Earth Angel's went crazy over my shooting. They stepped up the drive by attacks in other gang territories. They hit Pomona hard. The war was on. Bobby told me the Earth Angels had captured who they thought might be the triggerman in Pomona. He said they tortured him in a van and then killed him out in an abandoned parking lot. It honestly made me sick to my stomach to hear about it. I was left feeling sorry for the young guys whose lives were being lost, especially for the one they tortured. I'd come to find out later exactly who shot me, a murderous gang member called Damon. Damon bragged about shooting a kid in all of the bars like the real coward he was. The one who was tortured, though he was a 12th Street Shark gang member, was not this guy they called Damon. Revenge did not fill the void I sensed in my heart. I could not stop the EA's from responding.

I decided on my own I would completely forsake the gang life. I didn't have any guidance so I went about it on my own. I decided I would start by reading the Bible. I started with the Old Testament. I read about creation and the first several generations of God's people. I found I still had strong desires to join the many wild parties my mom and Ray would throw for the gang, on the other side of the door. I'd be inside my room reading the Bible, outside would be the gang taking drugs, drinking alcohol, all the while listening to the gangster toons (1960's music).

On one particular Friday they were having one of their regular parties at my house, Psycho and Chato, Vice

Prez of the Jr. EA's, confronted my brother Huero and told him to bring me outside so they could teach me a lesson for not being a part of the gang. He responded by standing up to them and telling them that the two of them would have to go through him first. As crazy as Psycho was he and Chato looked at each other and walked away. Huero had to answer to Santos the Prez later on, but Santos told him he would have done the same for his younger brother.

    I found myself torn. I wanted so bad to know more about God, to know Him personally if it were possible. I would read the law, about lust, about murder, about lying and so on. Finally one day as I was reading the Law of the Old Testament, the same voice I had heard out in the abandoned field spoke to my heart once again, pointing me in the right direction. I specifically heard the voice say, "You know, this is not the way", speaking about trying to earn salvation through obeying the law of the Old Testament. So I spoke out to this voice and asked, "Then, what is the way"? The voice of God or of an Angel, I do not know, replied, "Jesus is the way". I was stunned and at the same time I did not understand the full meaning of those words. I responded for the last time, "Well, I don't understand that, when I do understand, then I'll come to Him".

    You see, I thought I had to first clean up my life and change all my ways, before Jesus could accept me. However, it wasn't working. I seemed trapped by my own bad ways. I started hanging with James, a lawless drug user friend of mine. James was a Mexican immigrant who had taught himself English. I met him in the holding cell of the Ontario Police department a couple of years earlier. I figured at least he wasn't in a gang. I began lying and stealing to get money to buy drugs, namely PCP and LSD.

I also began drinking again. My mothers live in boyfriend Ray got a raise at work so they decided to move to a bigger house. We moved to a four-bedroom home. Ray made great promises about being a dad to us. However, the parties continued and grew worse. Terrible things started happening to the gang. It was time to reap what they had sowed for so many years.

At a gang meeting one Friday night the gang was gathered at their usual hang out. Everyone was sitting on a broken down brick wall in front of an old ladies house. Graffiti was sprawled all over. Two EA gang members were stationed as guards at different ends of the street with semi automatic rifles. It was at that time that an unmarked car (not a gangster's car) came driving down the street. The guards put their guns to the side.

When the car got to the end of the street it made a U-turn. The gang was unalarmed. After all, it was a beat up old car. As the car passed by the gang the second time, the windows of the car rolled down and the gang members inside of the car held their guns out the window and started blasting away with their guns at the EA's. Two of the Jr. EA's, named Frankie and Johnny, were hit. Frankie was rolling around the ground holding his stomach while Johnny was lying dead on the ground with a gunshot wound to the head. There was blood everywhere. Frankie grew up on this street and his home was next door to the old ladies house. His mom was home at the time of the shooting. Frankie died shortly thereafter. The weirdest part of the whole thing is out of all the gang members there that day Frankie and Johnny were childhood friends, having grown up on Monterey Street together. The logo of the Earth Angels was of the Grim Reeper, and they had spray painted the image of the Grim Reeper on the street in front of Frankie and Johnny's homes. The Grim Reeper came knocking and took these two boys out. The carload of gang members got away in the unmarked car.

  By this time, Bobby was close to seventeen years of age. He left home to stay with various gang friends, or different girl friends. He was heavily into the gang activity. He would come home once in a while. He was living a violent life. I would hear about all the violence going down, about different people being killed. He came to stay with us for a while during his junior year of High School. We went to the continuation high school up the street from our house. He was settling on a teen aged girl named Lori. She was the sister of one of the older EA's. The partying didn't stop for Bob, nor did the violence.

  After some time of staying away from the gang I grew bored. For whatever reason I thought it would be cool to go see my old friend Betty and her two sisters. My younger brother Jeff and my cousin Doug came along. I don't remember much about that day, but I do know it would be the last time I ever went there. We were all laughing and having a good time. We were trying to figure out what to do with the evening, but none of us had any cash.

  Later in the evening an older man came by, what they call a veteran gang member, with a Tupperware container full of every drug imaginable. This guy totally freaked me out. Not only was he carrying this container out in the open while walking around town, he was carrying a nickel-plated handgun out in the open as well. Not to mention he was using the drugs himself, he was way out there.

  I guess we told him we would try and get some money or perhaps we would buy next time, so he left the house moving backwards with his gun swinging to the right and left to make sure we didn't jump him for his stash. We didn't think too much about it after he left. We all went into Betty's room and sat on the bed, joking around and laughing. I was standing by the closet at the opposite end of the room.

There came a knock at the door later in the evening. Betty's mom answered the door to find this same strung out drug dealer standing there half-coherent. We all quieted to hear what was going on. She asked a couple of times what he wanted, until he finally asked her if she could give him a sock, as in a sock you wear on your foot. We couldn't believe our ears. He repeated it again, "ca, ca, can I ha, have a, um sock". I was worried about the whole thing. This guy was strung out with a loaded gun, a bad combination.

My friends on the other hand thought this was the funniest thing ever. They started making fun of the guy, repeating what he said and laughed hysterically. I knew it was a bad idea so I kept telling them to stop. Just then the old guy pushed Betty's mom out of the way and walked into the room with his gun. Betty's mom went into her own room without a care, all she ever did was party, that is pretty much all she lived for. Of course, I had never heard anything about Betty's dad.

When this guy walked into the room with his gun he didn't look at anyone except for me. He pointed his gun right at my face and asked me why I was making fun of him. I was mad at everyone but was unwilling to say it had been everyone else. I froze, I had already been shot and stabbed before, and here I was once again facing death. I started backing toward the closet very slowly, figuring I would jump inside, anything not to have that gun in my face.

Everyone in the room started apologizing to the guy and telling him the truth about how they had been the ones making fun of him and that I was trying to stop them. Fortunately he was coherent enough to understand. He put his gun down and then shook my hand and left. I was stunned and shaking. I scolded my friends and then my brother and cousin, thereafter, I left. After that I realized none of these friends were worth keeping. Hanging out with the gang and even the non-gang friends that were involved in drinking, partying, and drugs was not worth it. Therefore, I stayed home.

I started back in school, only this time it was at a continuation high school. Continuation is basically where they send you after you have been expelled from regular High School. It is where all the drug users and gang members went. Most of the girls there were young unwed-mothers. Some were gang types; most of them were drug users as well. The whole set up was you worked at your own pace and at your own level. It was the first time since elementary school that I enjoyed learning and felt I was learning something meaningful. I did well in the classes, especially in the art classes.

I still felt the same nagging emptiness inside. Things at home were still pretty bad. My mom and Ray were still having wild parties. Not only that, but they were also selling drugs and had been for sometime. Our new home was still the party place for the EA's. The last party I can remember was terrible. It must have been my sister Helen's birthday or something. She and my mom went out to the wineries in Guasti, near Rancho Cucamonga, to buy literally cases of bottled wine.

All night the gangsters drank the wine and played billiards, dancing in the empty formal dining room. I drank a little, but for the most part the whole thing bothered me. One of the gang members confronted me and asked why I hadn't been attending the gang meetings. I told him it was because of my wounds. He asked me what I was doing at the party. I grew tired of it and got in his face and told him the obvious, "I live here". My mom was dancing seductively with one of the gang members. I looked over at Ray, he was ready to rip the guys head off. My brother Huero and I looked at each other as if to ask whether or not to beat the crap out of or maybe even kill our fellow gang member for this disrespect.

The dancing stopped. We were ashamed of our own mother. Huero was so upset and strung out he yelled at her and told everyone he was going to go outside to commit suicide. They knew he wasn't kidding so most of the older gang members followed him to stop him, which they did. By this time I went to bed. I was disgusted with the whole thing. Sometime late that evening one of the girls brought over some LSD. The girls and some of the guys smoked the stuff. Soon afterwards several of them overdosed. They started totally freaking out. I don't remember if they were rushed to the hospital or not. That was the worst party experience any of us ever had. It was the last party they would have at our house. Things kept getting worse for the gang as well as for my family.

Gary and Martin, the two brothers who lived next door to my family in the projects where I grew up both joined the EA's gang as well. They were unable to move outside of the projects, and were the most unlikely gang members.

I figure the only reason they joined was for the protection of the gang from other gangs in the area. Joining the gang would end in great tragedy for one of the brothers. As they were going inside their parent's apartment, a Junior Black Angel, who went by the name Crook came out from behind a fence, pulled out a gun and started shooting for Gary. He ended up shooting Martin once in the back. Sadly, Martin died instantly. Crook ran like the coward he was, like so many cowards who shoot young people while they wait in hiding or as they shoot from inside a moving car. Martin was not a hated gang member, not even by the rival gangs. He also had some relatives in the Black Angels as well as a lot of friends. The Funeral was sad. His parents were understandably distraught, as were his two younger sisters.

  The EA's had the audacity to show up at the funeral, and as a group knelt before Martin's casket, all together performing the sign of the cross. Many of the Black Angels showed up as well.   It felt like a scene straight out of a Mafia movie.   Gary's non-gang friends and family were distraught and visibly upset by the gang's presence, yet were unwilling to say anything. I was no longer active in the gang; I only showed up for Martin's funeral.

  The EA's gang did not retaliate against Crook's gang because the leaders of the Senior Black Angels secretly assured the leaders of the EA's that Crook would be taken care of. Crook was a loner and picked the wrong family to carry out a vendetta against. As it turned out Crook acted alone, without the approval of his gang's leaders, and so within a week or so from the funeral, Crook was hanging out with Oso, a fellow gang member who Crook trusted from the Jr. Black Angels. They decided to kick back at

Oso's house. Late that night, Crook was leaning against a window in Oso's bedroom. Immediately after Oso left Crook alone in his room, someone lying in wait outside of the window shot Crook through the glass at point blank range right in the head. He died instantly. No one knew who shot him. My brother Huero wouldn't say. Finally, some time later Huero confidentially told me that it was the Sr. Black Angels that killed Crook, one of their own.

The Earth Angels stopped coming around my house altogether. It was a good thing. My mom and Ray, however, didn't change. Things had gotten so out of hand with my parents in relation to the level of violence my step dad showed toward our mom that my two brothers and I almost killed Ray. I am saddened by the memory of this and am glad it did not end in bloodshed. Ray thought my mom was having an affair on him. She had left the house early one day to go to a girl friends house for the day. When she came back he was drunk and had a loaded 22-caliber rifle waiting. I was standing there inside the house feeling pretty helpless. Huero went next door to borrow a 22 rifle, which they lent him. When my mom pulled up in her Toyota Corolla, she stayed inside the car. Ray shot at her twice, hitting the car. They started arguing as they usually did. These arguments were usually all out fights frequently turning violent. He put the gun away and she came inside. He kept accusing her of cheating on him; she swore she was at a friend's house. He grabbed a steak knife and chased her into the bathroom. She stayed in there crying with him on the other side of the door. By this time Huero returned with the loaded rifle as he handed it to us through the window. My brother Jeff and I had aluminum baseball bats. We were ready and willing to kill

Ray to end the violence against our family. I asked Huero what the plan was. He said if Ray tried to get into the bathroom with the knife we would all come out at once and start shooting and beating him with the bats. I pictured Ray picking up his rifle and returning fire. It was truly scary.

Our adrenaline was pumping. We were ready to go, waiting and perhaps hoping Ray would make his next move. The years of abuse toward our mom and toward us had been too much for any of us to handle. Ray finally left her alone. He put the knife away and left. We put our weapons away. Huero never returned the rifle to our neighbor; he kept it for the EA's stash of weapons.

After that, along with the terrible things going on with the gang, things seemed to quiet down in our house. My brother Bobby started bringing a young married couple to our house to play billiards and have a beer or two, nothing more than that. They were close friends of Bobby's girl friend Lori. His name was Dan and his wife's name was Cindy. He was white; he had long blond hair, and blue eyes like Bobby. His wife Cindy was a very pretty, nice Hispanic lady. Each time they came over I couldn't help but notice a real difference in their lives. Dan was not involved in gang's in any way.

They had this look of fulfillment or something in their eyes and in their expressions. They did not have many possessions or a lot of money; they were trying to make ends meet like most newly married couples. Yet they seemed so content with life, like they had a reason to live. After getting to know them for sometime I began to get a glimpse as to what this difference in their lives was all about. I couldn't help but ask them questions about it. It grabbed my interest and touched something inside of me.

That void inside of our hearts most of us feel deep down inside had somehow been filled up completely in Dan and Cindy's lives.

I started looking forward to the times they would come over; playing pool, listening to Rock n' Roll, and talking about God. Dan and his wife were real people, not plastic or fake. They shared with me about how there is more to life than simply believing God exists. They explained how I could have a personal friendship with Jesus Christ and this is what He desired for us all. They explained at my request how Jesus' death on the cross made it possible for not only my sins to be forgiven, but also how I could know Christ. He would be a part of my life, and fill the void in my heart, giving me a hope and a reason for living. It hit me like a ton of bricks that this is exactly what I had been searching for. I knew this was everything I wanted. Exactly what Dan and his wife had.

Dan invited me to attend church with them on the following Sunday. I was happy to go. The weekend came and was unusually quiet. My parents didn't drink and no gang members came over. Sunday finally arrived. Dan and Cindy stopped by to pick me up. The church was pretty big and filled with a lot of people. The Minister of the church was a short man with white hair named Daniel. He was what they called a fireball preacher. When he preached he would get excited, moving his arms up and down, speaking loudly about the eternal truths God gave him to share with the people in church. Dan and his wife had something that meant everything to them in their lives, and now this preacher was excited about the same thing, the opportunity to have a personal relationship with Jesus Christ.

Reverend Daniel shared about how we could openly talk to Christ and how Christ would minister back to us in different ways. Through Christ's death on a cross we could receive complete forgiveness for our sins. Moreover, here was the clincher for me; we did not need to change our lives before Jesus would accept us. Although we do need to turn away from living a sinful life, we aren't required to overcome sin and wrongdoing before coming to Christ; Christ would accept us as we are, sin and all. The preacher gave an open invitation to whoever wanted to accept Christ in their lives, to come down to the front of the church.

I didn't hesitate for a second. I went down to the front of the church with several others. I heard a lot of clapping from the church. We were escorted to a side room of the church, where men and women counselors met us. I spoke with a counselor and he explained to me in more detail about Christ's death and Resurrection from the dead, and about forgiveness and knowing Christ. We prayed together, and as we prayed I felt a weight being lifted off of my shoulders. The prayer went something like this: "Dear Lord Jesus, I believe you are the Son of God and you rose from the grave. Please forgive me for my sins and please forgive me for being a sinner. I repent from living a life of sin. Please help me to know you more and to honor you with my life. Thank you for saving me and for coming into my heart, in Jesus' name, Amen." Somehow blinders had been taken off my eyes; I could see the truth. Finally, for the first time in my life I felt fulfilled; the void in my heart had finally been filled with the love and acceptance of Jesus Christ. I finally received the promise God had made to me when I was dying out in the field with multiple gunshot and stab wounds. There is a reason to live; there truly is hope. God kept His promise to me and introduced me to His Son Jesus Christ, the true meaning and true hope in life.

The counselor helped me to understand the importance to nurture my new relationship with Christ. Just as a newborn baby needs to eat and grow, so does our spirit within us. The more we know Christ, the more we grow. Going to church and regularly reading the Bible became very important to me. When I came out of the room I came out a new person with a new heart, I felt like I was walking on clouds. I later found out the reason the people in the church got so excited and started clapping was they had been praying for me for weeks. Their prayers, and mine, had been answered. Our God is an awesome God.

Jesus Christ performed a miracle in our neighborhood. After a few years many of the Black Angel and Earth Angel gang members would come to know Christ, including my older sister Helen and brother Bobby. Many lives had been touched, and many stories of triumph have come about as a result. A lot of the former members, including myself, have stuck with our newfound relationship with Christ. For me personally, receiving Jesus Christ as my personal Lord and Savior has been the single most important decision in my life, setting the stage for a great and prosperous future; giving me a future and a hope.

R.K. Jensen

SEPARATE ROADS

My brother Bobby started attending church with Dan and Cindy as well. Yet, he had a harder time wholeheartedly embracing his newfound faith. He went to church on and off with his steady girl friend Lori. Sadly, it was short lived because he wouldn't stop hanging out with the gang members. It is a lesson hard learned by many drug addicts and gang members, as hard as it is, he and the others that wanted to change needed to cut all ties to the gangs and people who take and sell the drugs. As a result of continuing to hang around the old crowd, the seed of faith in his heart was stolen away. When the opportunity came to move up in the ranks of the gang, he went for it and stopped attending church altogether. At the same time many of the Black Angels and the Earth Angels were embracing faith, the Senior Earth Angel's decided it was time for the Jr. EA's Gang to graduate to the next level. The Senior Earth Angels Gang are the ones who started the Jr. Earth Angels to begin with. These men were in their late twenties and early thirties. Many of them were also members of the Mexican Mafia. The leaders told my brother Bobby if he came back to the gang he would be made Vice President of the newly reorganized senior gang. It was all he needed to leave the church and fall back into gangs.

The Jr. EA's once again had to go through an initiation process before they could become part of the senior gang. The initiation involved following an assignment. This time it went beyond beating up on each other to see who was tough and who wasn't. These assignments were straight out of the pit of hell. All of these assignments involved carrying out a contract on someone's life, which means to kill people the gang had grudges against. These assignments were carried out against ordinary people not related to gangs, as well as gang members from rival gangs. My friend Joe, the one I had originally discouraged from joining the Junior EA's, confided in me he was sorry he had joined. He did not want to carry out his assignment against a young white man who was ordered dead because the young white man confronted some of the Senior EA's and pride-fully told them the gang was all about nothing. Joe and two other gang members were to ambush the man at his home in the quiet of the evening and then shoot him through a window. I didn't ask if he carried out the assignment, however, if Joe did not carry it out, then he possibly could have been killed.

Prison wasn't too far off for Bobby. His actions and bad decisions caught up with him. He was arrested for various gang related crimes, and as a repeat offender, he was sentenced to do hard time in the State and Federal Prisons. He spent time in Fulsome, and San Quentin, two of the hardest prisons housing some of the Nations deadliest criminals. He told me there were times when he would get into so much trouble in those prisons he was put in solitary confinement. He said it was a small square room with thick walls and a door with a small square hole for a window, if that, and a toilet on the wall. It was very dark, lonely, and cold. He said he would exercise and sleep. As tough as Bobby had become, I knew being locked up had to be a hard thing.

Every so often Bobby would get out and pay a visit.

The more time he served, the less I knew or recognized him. He changed dramatically. His looks changed. He became a hardened convict. He had tattoo markings on most of his arms, back, and forehead. His speech was noticeably different as well. It became difficult to understand him. He spoke in a sub-culture language of combined slang Spanish with slang English, which was spoken in broken sentences. Some sort of prison slang used to communicate with each other in the prison system. He blamed God for his experiences in prison. Sadly, he doubted Jesus loved him at all. I knew this because of the time he struggled through his tears as he attempted to ask me if there were a God, how could God let him get beat down so bad in Prison. Up until that moment, I had no idea how bad it was in prison for my older brother.

He unfolded the story about when he first entered the prison system; he was left alone in a holding cell with a hardened convict twice his size. The man threatened him and gave him mean looks. He knew he couldn't take this guy, yet he also knew what this guy had in mind. This man was going to beat Bobby down simply because he didn't like the way Bob looked. So Bobby walked up to the guy and slugged him as hard as he could in the face, knowing even if he didn't win, at least he would establish respect with the prisoners as one who did not back down. The man didn't even flinch. He wiped the floor with my brother so bad that he was put in the Prison hospital. He questioned any ounce of faith left inside of him.

It was around this time in prison that Bobby, a.k.a. Huero, joined the Mexican Mafia, and otherwise referred to as the Eme. Blade, our dad, did not approve of his decision. Blade, himself a member of the Arian Brotherhood, otherwise known as the white mob, told Huero not to join the Mexican Mafia. He told Huero that because he was white in race, despite that he had some Hispanic blood in him, the Mexican Mafia would only use him. Make promises and never deliver because they considered him to be a gavacho, or a white man. Despite the warnings from Blade, he joined the Mexican Mafia. I honestly think he joined to upset Blade, paying him back for the years of abandonment and abuse.

Bobby was given training and materials on how to be a cold-blooded assassin, or a hit man. He was issued weapons. He became skilled as an assassin. Whenever they needed someone killed, he would methodically carry it out, without so much as a trace of his presence. He carried out these assignments not only within the prison system, but also when he was out on the streets. I hesitantly asked him what being a hit man was about while he was out of jail. He told me what made him the best. In so many words he told me that he would covertly (secretly) stalk the person the mafia had a contract on. He would follow them around for days or weeks at a time, getting to know their every move. When the timing was right he would strike without anyone ever knowing he was even there. It shook me inside to know what my brother had become.

The Mexican Mafia made him Sergeant of Arms. In this position he was responsible for holding and hiding all of the weapons in the prison for the Mexican Mafia. He made use of the constant flow of Mafia girl friends, visitors, as well as crooked guards to obtain and hide these various weapons. Huero had guns, zip guns, and shanks (homemade stabbing devices made of metals and razor sharp materials) hidden within the walls of the prison, in his cell, and in the cells of other inmates. Eventually, I lost touch with Bob. I was unable to keep a close relationship with him because his activities involved Mafia assignments. One thing I did learn about the Mob is you don't ever want to ask for a favor from any member. Guaranteed, they will come knocking at your door expecting something very bad in return, or else. Nothing is done for free.

    Snoop and Freddie, the two friends who were with me the night I was shot and stabbed did not escape the hardships of the ghetto. Even though they saw first hand what happened to me in the field the night I was attacked, they still made the wrong choices. Snoop ended up joining the Black Angel's along with his two older brothers. They would learn the hard way that the only sure outcome of gang life is a grim future that guarantees prison time, becoming physically disabled, or death. Not too long after, Snoop's older brother was shot in a drive by shooting, ending up paralyzed for life. Snoop became a drug addict. He was murdered when the drug dealer he bought drugs from purposely gave him a poisoned dose of the drug. Freddie never did join a gang, but continued to hang around them. He must have upset the wrong people. Freddie was at his mom's home one day when a carload of gang members came by asking for him. He must have known them well because he went up to the car and stuck his head inside the window. Without warning, they took out a gun and shot him point blank in the head. Leaving him for dead in broad daylight he died right in front of his mom's house.

    Despite many opportunities to build their faith in Christ, Bob and the others, including Helen, continued to live the street life. The end result of their actions and decisions would soon be realized. Families and friends would pay the price because a loved one is hurt, imprisoned, or worse yet killed in an untimely death as a direct result of living for parties, drugs, crime, gangs, and the Mafia; the only absolute future for anyone who lives this way.

Nothing about the gang life appealed to me any more. The addictions I had to various types of drugs and alcohol, even smoking, was gone for good. Jesus set me free from the chains of sin and miraculously delivered me from drugs and alcohol by bringing my spirit to life, giving me a new heart, and renewing my mind through His word the Bible. Whenever the church doors were opened I was there. When I wasn't doing homework for High School, I was praying and reading the Bible. It was a good change for me. I had truly been delivered from the bonds of sin over my life. The Lord spared me from going through the agony my brother Bobby, along with these gang members and ex-gang members had put themselves through. Jesus Christ put a spiritual covering of protection around my life that is with me to this day.

With the gang out of my life I was able to concentrate on my new life as a Christian. I had made a conscious decision to stay away from them. I wouldn't visit old friends from the gang, nor would I ask to go along with Bob or Helen to their get-togethers with the gang. I didn't think or act like I was better than any of them. On the contrary, I wasn't any better. Nothing the gang life had to offer could compare to the joy and inner peace I had found in my relationship with Christ. Not the parties, the cruising, the dates, or the false sense of pride that went along with the whole lifestyle. In contrast, I had found something worth living for, even worth dying for.

As time went by, such a large number of the newly

formed Earth Angel's put their faith in Christ that the gang of about 175 members disbanded in the mid 1980's; never to be re-started again. Even the ladies version disbanded. This was good for the community, and it was good for those who like me put their faith into practice. Yet putting our faith into practice proved to be somewhat of a challenge. This was a brand new way of living for all of us. Several churches in the area took on the task of assisting us in our newfound faith. A lot of the former gang members of both the EA's and the Black Angels attended Victory Outreach. I knew God wanted me at the Assembly of God church on the North Side of town where I first accepted Christ; only there were no former gang members in the church I was attending.

Attending a wealthy all white church had its challenges. The adults readily accepted me. Some of the adults had made a commitment to being there for me, to help me make the transition from the gang life to a more productive one. I had a lot to learn. Not only about my new found faith, but also about life in general. Fitting in the youth group at the church was a different story altogether. I could sense the prejudice from some of the teens in the group. Unfortunately, they were the main teens in the youth group. At that point I didn't care too much about it. I wasn't going to church for their friendship; I was going to learn about Christ. Some of the kids were nice and accepting of me, yet they were much younger than I was. That made it a little easier. After a while Dan and Cindy, the young couple who originally invited me to church, told me they would no longer be able to pick me up for church. I was a little discouraged; being my house was a long walk to the church. Rather than stay discouraged, I had determined I would continue to go to the church even if I had to walk every Sunday and Wednesday evening. There was nothing worth going back to on the streets. The changes in my life wouldn't come easy, overcoming obstacles would be hard, yet I was learning that anything worth this much was not going to come easily, that nothing is worth more than the freedom and love of Jesus Christ.

Come Sunday morning, I'd get dressed in the only clothes I had, gang type clothing. I'd grab my little pocket Bible the Church gave me and start walking to Church. I called it my switchblade Bible because I could conceal it in my back pocket. I would arrive to greetings from several of the adults and the Church staff. I could tell they were genuinely interested in seeing me. A few of the youth were glad to see me as well; however, as mentioned these youth were much younger than I was. The teens that were my age ignored me. Bigotry was alive and thriving in the Church. Not everyone was like that. Yet it did not belong there, not in church of all places. After a few months of this I became discouraged. I hadn't made any close friends in the youth group. Despite it all, I kept going to Church on a regular basis.

Pretty soon I was arriving at Church discouraged, as I felt so lonely. As a gang member I had all the friends I wanted and they seemed to be happy to see me whenever I was around. They call it being down with the homies, or down with the hood. However, the friendships in the "hood" are totally on the surface, or fake; based on gang ties. The moment you mess up you are ousted and beaten. Then they accept you again. If you mess up bad you could end up dead by your so-called friends. Bottom line, gang types don't have friendships in the true sense of the word.

I felt like perhaps leaving the church and do what, I did not know. I needed a miracle. The following Sunday Reverend Daniel preached a good message. He gave an invitation for anyone who needed prayer to come up to the front of the church for prayer. I went to the front and kneeled down and prayed. In my private prayer I spoke to Jesus about how I felt as though His Church had rejected me, as a result I was feeling rejected by Christ Himself. As I was pouring my heart out to God in prayer, a man sitting in a seat nearby was thumbing through his Bible and then got up and walked directly behind me. He told me God had spoken to his heart to give me a message directly from Jesus, just for me. That got my full attention. He shared with me these words on God's behalf: "I the Lord Jesus personally accept you into my family". God ministered to my heart in the most awesome way. I cried and thanked Jesus through my tears for meeting me in a special way. I felt like a ton of bricks were released off my shoulders.

    This man had no way of knowing what I was going through. I had never met him before, and come to think of it, I don't ever remember seeing him again after that. I hadn't shared how I was feeling with Reverend Daniel, or anyone else for that matter. I had never had anyone share a word from Jesus with me before this. I do remember how blessed I was. To know Jesus Christ has personally accepted me into His family. I found the inner strength I needed to press on in my relationship with Christ. I have got to say in the same way Christ accepts me you have got to know He accepts you and loves you completely. No matter what your past, no matter how anyone else has mistreated you or rejected you, you are welcomed by Him, He will never turn you away. It also helped to understand

Jesus had every intention of meeting me half way in my efforts to know Him. The Bible clearly states that as we grow closer to God, He in turn moves closer to us and is better able to bless us with all of our needs and even some of our hearts desires, according to His will. What could be better than that?

I kept going to the church despite the problems. Sometime later, most of the youth warmed up to me and became friends. I even went on to become a leader in the youth group. One of the older youth from the church apologized for not liking me because of my race. His dad was one of the Pastors of the church. After getting to know me, he realized I was no different than anyone else. He said God had dealt with his heart about his attitude. He realized if he couldn't love someone he could see with his own eyes, how ever could he say he truly loved God who he could not see with these same physical eyes. Overall it didn't matter if some of the church members had a hang up about race or the color of my skin. Nor did it matter that people felt awkward about having an ex-gang member regularly coming to church. None of that mattered, Jesus personally accepted me. The miracle of Jesus speaking to my heart through this man of faith solidified my faith, making it much stronger, helping to prepare me for unforeseen future hardships and trials that are to take place in my life in the many months and years ahead; trials that were met with many miracles and answers to prayer.

BEYOND BELIEF

Psalms 27:10   "When my father and mother forsake me, then the Lord will take care of me."

"You won't make it through regular High School". That is what my counselor said to me at the continuation high school I was attending. I asked her opinion about going back to the regular High School to finish my diploma the right way. She took me by surprise with her response. Instead of becoming discouraged I smiled and became more determined to accomplish my new goal.

The following week I was sitting in the office of Mr. Vargas, the man who would be my counselor at Ontario High School. I remember him telling me with disbelief I was an entire year behind with my credits. He was unaware that I missed a whole year of school because of my wounds. He knew I was determined to attend regular School, so he gave me the choice between starting off as a sophomore, and forgetting about the lost credits, or to start off as a junior, with a years worth of credits to catch up on. I chose the sophomore standing and started on an exciting course in my life.

It didn't take too long to catch up with the other students. Initially I had trouble with some subjects, math in particular. Like any other student I had my strengths and weaknesses. I did quite well in literature, science, and especially the arts. For the first time in years I was enjoying my education. Learning was a challenge, yet at the same time fun and rewarding.

I was finally learning what a normal life was about. The more I learned the more I enjoyed school. I was experiencing a life full of purpose, and full of meaning. Knowing I could have and accomplish goals. I was driven to do well. I spent all of my time in School, at home doing homework, practicing the flute for band, or going to church. At church I became involved in a ministry called Royal Rangers as a Junior Commander. This is a boy's program designed to reach, teach, and keep boys for Christ through camping activities and Bible stories, somewhat similar to the Boy Scouts. The men who served as leaders became my mentors.

Many of the leaders in the Royal Rangers were business owners. At times they would hire me to do odd jobs. It wasn't that I needed the money; it was that the leaders were going out of their way to be there for me. Some of the men were previously in the party and drug scene before accepting Christ. There were some who had been Christians since childhood. I learned a lot about life from each of these men and their families.

Lance, the main leader of the Royal Rangers at the time, went out of his way to be there for me. He was a true "big brother". He had a story to tell about his life. He had a dramatic testimony. Yet, what I remember most about him was he put love into action. He was there to listen, to encourage, and to help me grow. It was nice to see men who had faced similar struggles as myself; they were now living good lives with wonderful families. I had hope for the future. These men didn't treat me like I was some ignorant minority gang member, they treated me as though I were a son or at the least a friend. It was nice considering the fact that at my home I didn't have parents that cared whatsoever.

By this time in my life my mother's boy friend Ray had lost his job at the Bait Factory. His party life was catching up to him. He was hung over at work and fell asleep on the job. He allowed the boilers to overheat, nearly blowing up the factory. Once again we had to move. The house had two bedrooms, one bathroom, and a small kitchen, with a small living room. That was it. My bed was the couch in the living room. There was a small Baptist church down the street from the house, at the end of the block. My Grandma lived across the street from us, in a similarly small home. My mom and Ray had four children together, a boy and three girls. The three girls were the prettiest little girls you would ever see. They had beautiful smiles and lots of laughs. Sadly, all seven of us lived in this small home. Bobby was in adult prison. My younger brother Jeff was living with his girlfriend.

When my mom and Ray were home all they would do was argue and fight. If they weren't fighting because they were drugged out and drunk, they were fighting when they were sober. I had a neighbor come over and tell me I should leave home for good before I went crazy. And it was crazy. At times I felt like I was the only string holding what was left of our family together.

At church I became a good friend with an Indonesian teen named James. He was a part of the Royal Rangers program. His parents Jim and Malahli accepted me as a part of their family. Jim was kind enough to allow me to be a part of his home and at the same time give me advice and hard to hear correction from time to time. Jim was from Australia and was now a successful businessman here in America. He got mixed up in drugs as a young man, then gave his life to Christ and was changed for the good. Malahli was a beautiful Indonesian woman. She was educated and the sweetest person you would ever meet. Jim was the director of a National Prison Ministry at the time. Jim invited me to speak with him as a guest speaker. This would be the first time I would publicly share my story. How I had wished I had been born to Jim and Malahli. They treated me like a son. I would spend the night and eat dinner there frequently. Malahli was like the mom I never had. She was such a sweet and caring person. Their home was a place of solace during hard times.

     Whenever my parents argued I would go to the other room and start singing worship songs I had learned at church. A peace would well up within my heart and soul. I would have a peace that surpassed all understanding, and I would know everything was going to be all right. After singing a song or two, my parents would stop arguing. Christ was my strength and His peace was wisdom to my Soul. On top of the strict poverty and violence in the home, I still had severe asthma to deal with. I was on a regular regimen of medication for the asthma. No, life's problems didn't disappear when I gave my heart to Christ, although He helps me through them, and at times delivers me from them altogether. One time I was so stressed I accidentally took two doses of my medication. My heart was pounding and fluttering. I felt sick. It was time to go to sleep, and I had to get up early for school the next day. I prayed and told the Lord I was having an adverse reaction. Immediately my heartbeat returned to normal, and I felt an inner peace. I quickly fell to sleep and had a restful sleep that evening.

Ray's alcoholism became worse. He gave me a hard time for going to church. He even told me not to read his Catholic Bible. He became verbally abusive toward me, cussing at me and saying degrading things. On one particular day I was doing homework and working on some training materials for the Royal Rangers. Ray was outside getting drunk. Before I could finish the assignment Ray came to the screen door with a mean look on his face as he called my name. He said, "Ron, come outside, I'm going to kill you". I sat there with my mouth dropped open. My mom was sitting next to me. She screamed realizing he was not joking. She immediately ran up to the door and slammed it in his face. With her back to the door and some super human strength she kept him from getting inside. There must have been an Angel helping her. I was so taken by surprise by the whole thing all I could do was sit there in shock. He finally left the house for the night.

Not too long after that occasion, on one particular night, Ray was drunk, when he decided to drive his Pontiac Trans Am to get more beer. He didn't come home. He ended up in the hospital after hitting an old truck head on. His car was totaled and he lost all of his front teeth on the metal chain steering wheel he had installed in the car. Fortunately no one was in the truck. Ironically, Ray left me alone after that.

My mom eventually gave her life to Jesus Christ and started going to the church with me. The kids came along as well. Several months later, Ray started going to church as well. He and my mom eventually married. Jim and Malahli were the best man and maid of honor. We still lived in the small home, yet things seemed to be looking much better. I was doing well at school, excelling in the arts, literature, and sciences, although, I still had a hard time with math. In short, I was beating the odds. At school I became involved in student government and I was the President of the Ontario High School Art Club. I also helped start the Ontario High School Christian Club.

Things were looking much better at home, however it would be short lived. The overwhelming odds and circumstances proved to be too much for some. There were drugs being sold not just nearby my home, yet even out of my home by my parents once again. I remember finding out my mom was dealing the drug heroine from our home. I had no idea she was a dealer. I was busy with school and church. I saw my life as becoming more ideal. Then I found out. I thought she was going to church a changed person. I found out by accident as I was walking through the living room one day, only to witness my mom standing at the front door, she took money from the man standing outside and in turn gave him a balloon filled with drugs. I felt so betrayed. I contacted the Youth Pastor of my church. He suggested getting out of the house as soon as I could. I didn't see how it was possible. So I stuck it out as best as I could. And I did it. The odds were totally against me in every way. Those are the odds the Lord loves to beat. Through it all Jesus was there for me. He never let me down. He didn't allow the gang to harm me. He didn't allow Ray in his drunkenness to harm me. Moreover, even though I was crushed when I discovered my mom had stopped going to church and started selling drugs, the Lord healed my wounded heart and I was able to press on.

At home and at school I would share my story and the love of Christ with any and everyone I could. I felt strongly about sharing my faith. When I was in the gang a couple of years earlier, there were a lot of younger kids who looked up to the older gang members. Just as I had looked up to the gangsters before I joined. People who knew me from my gang days noticed the change in my life. Two of the kids from the neighborhood I know for sure looked up to gangs were named Donny and Jesse. They were 11 or 12 years old at the time. They knew me from the gang days. Both of these kids were on their way to becoming gang members. Jesse's mom was a drug user and his uncle was a drug dealer and user as well. He lived on the corner in a shack. Donny lived across the street from Jesse. Donny partied a lot with older guys. He was a lot worse off than Jesse was.

  I had an opportunity to sit down and tell Donny about my story. I reminded Donny about my past and shared with him the awesome changes Christ had made in my life. I went through the Bible with him. I didn't hit him over the head with the Bible; I was never pushy about my faith. Don said he wasn't ready to accept Christ. Sure he believed Christ was real, yet he said he wasn't ready to stop partying. He felt he was too young and had a lot of years ahead of him. I had a strong impression he needed to accept Christ today. That he may not live past tomorrow. It was clear to me; there was no doubt in my mind what the Lord Jesus was speaking to my heart about. Therefore, I told Donny exactly what was on my heart. Again Donny told me how he enjoyed the parties and he had a lot of time ahead of him. Once again, Christ spoke to my heart, instructing me to once again tell him it was serious; we never know when we will die. This could be his last chance to accept Jesus as his Savior. So I told Donny just that. Sadly, Donny declined. Jesus spoke to my heart once again, telling me to let it go; I could not make him accept Christ. I prayed for Donny after he had left.

  The very next day Donny went to a party with a group of older men. Everyone was drinking. Donny got into an argument with one of the men. The man left the house and came back with a loaded gun. He shot Donny in the head. Donny died instantly. The Lord loved Donny so much He went out of His way to save him from this tragedy. The worst part of the whole thing is that Don's dad went to my church; only he didn't live the life or walk the talk of a committed Christian. Don's dad was a "secret" alcoholic. It didn't do any good for him to tell his kids how to live, when he lived opposite to what he was trying to teach his kids. Actions always speak louder than words.

  I took the opportunity to sit down with Jesse one day. Jesse is the boy who lived in the shack on the corner of the street, with his drug user mom. I spoke to Jesse about Christ's love and about the wonderful changes Christ has done in my life. I asked Jesse if he wanted to accept Christ into his heart. I was surprised when he said yes. We prayed together, and Jesse genuinely received Christ into his heart and became a child of God. He started going to church and reading his Bible. His mom and uncle didn't change. He still had to live in the shack. Yet he remained faithful. Christ was quite real to Jesse. Then about a year or so later, the car he was riding in got into a bad accident. Jesse died in the accident, at the age of fourteen. The good news is to this day and for the rest of eternity Jesse is in Heaven with His Lord and Savior, and I guarantee you he isn't living in a shack.

I went into the little neighborhood store down the street from our small home, with the intent to share my story with the elderly lady who worked in the store. I asked her very politely if I could take a moment to share with her about Jesus Christ. She startled me when she started clapping her hands and shouting for joy. She said to me, "I'm so blessed by your wanting to share the Lord with me. Did you know that while you were dying in the hospital after you were shot and stabbed, your grandmother came to our church and asked us to pray for you? We called everyone on the phone and prayed for you for the entire week. And here you are telling me about Jesus. Well, praise the Lord." I had always wondered who had prayed for me while I was in the hospital. I remembered how the Doctors were surprised how quickly I recovered. Now I knew. It was the prayer of the elderly women from the little Baptist Church down the street from my house; thank you grandma, and thank you Lord. The Lord works in wonderful ways.

  I was determined as ever to make this work. There was nothing to go back to. I was doing well in school. I had new friends who cared about education and goals for the future. I was learning a lot and enjoying life; not having to look over my shoulder and wonder whether or not I was going to be shot. I obtained a driver's license and had a part time job after school. For the most part I used a ten-speed bike during the summers to get to my summer job. When I was old enough to drive, my friend Rhonda taught me how to drive her Toyota. I began praying for a car of my own. I didn't earn enough to buy one. Being in High School didn't afford me the time to work full time. My mom and Ray certainly couldn't afford to buy me one, much less loan me the money for one. So I turned to the Lord. The Bible states that God will supply all my needs and I shouldn't worry because He knows full well what I have need of. This is a hard lesson to learn when you are living in poverty. I felt a car was more than a want; I needed one to make it to both work and school.

The last few times I prayed about the car situation I would have an impression to ask a certain family at church about helping out with this need, yet I didn't want to impose on anyone. Besides, what if I was wrong and they said absolutely not. I kept praying. Finally it clicked, the answer to my prayer was right there all along. The Lord showed me that the wealth He had blessed this family with belonged to Him. He not only blessed them for their families needs, but to help meet others needs as well. It was hard to do. What made it even harder was my good friend from church was a member of this dear family. Her name was Mandy. Her dad was a wealthy businessman. He drove a classic Corvette and Mandy would take his other convertible around town for fun. Funny thing about Mandy and her family though, their wealth never went to their heads. They were a loving family. Whenever I went over to their home they seemed as down to earth as anyone else I had met before. Mandy's dad was one of the leaders in the Royal Rangers. This is how I met him and his family. It was hard to do; yet I told him a little about my situation, nervously of course. Then I asked if he could possibly help me out with transportation.

The following week Mandy's dad had me meet them at the Department of Motor Vehicles. He met me there with Mandy's car. He gave me the keys and wrote down on the DMV papers that it was a gift. It was such a blessing. It was such an awesome answer to prayer. All I had to pay for was the insurance. How did Mandy feel about giving up her car? I think she felt blessed when her dad gave her keys to a Mercedes Benz he had bought from a Doctor friend of his. I don't think anyone felt as though I was taking advantage. Mandy's dad could see I was working hard at my studies and at work.

The day finally came when I graduated from regular High School as a member of the National Honor Roll; I received various Art awards, and graduated at the top 20% of the class. I went to Prom night, Grad night and my Graduation ceremony; being the first in my family to graduate from High School; awards and merits of honor, made this all the more special. My mom came by herself to the awards ceremony as well as to my graduation.

I could have given up. I had every reason one uses when they drop out of school; to include the violent and destitute situation at home I was faced with every day. On graduation day my mom gave me a couple hundred dollars. I didn't know where she got the money but I didn't want to refuse it on such a special day. I knew she was telling me she was proud of me the best way she knew how. I gave her a hug and said thank you. It was a good feeling to celebrate my graduation, but an even better feeling knowing how much I meant to the Lord. The Lord is truly a parent to the parentless.

I was accepted at a private University in Costa Mesa, California. My last day of High School was on a Friday. The next day I was at Southern California College taking the ACT test. Southern California College is an Assemblies of God Bible College. College life was a big change. I met some nice young people, and learned a great deal. God was there for me at every turn. I then changed schools and went to North West College closer to home. I graduated with perfect attendance and top grades. I went back to Calvary Church, the same Assembly of God I attended as a youth.

I became an assistant to the Youth Pastor, helping out with the Junior and Senior High group. I was also in charge of putting together the Youth Group bulletin. I met an eighteen-year old young lady named Anne in the Youth Group. Anne was coming with her younger sister Jan. All the guys were talking about them. I have to admit Anne first caught my eye when she was in the Youth Center sitting at the Piano playing a song. She didn't know it at the time, but I had hoped she would volunteer to assist with graphic arts projects when I mentioned needing help with the bulletin for the Youth Group. She volunteered and we became friends. Anne became more involved in the youth group and started growing in her faith.

The Lord met me in very special ways. His presence was real. He spoke clearly to my heart. Although, to be honest I had some doubt at times. I was puzzled that other people of faith didn't seem to have this type of closeness to the Lord. I had learned early on that as I drew near to Christ, He would draw near to me. Knowing Christ wasn't something I had to do on my own. He met me half way. Indeed, my entire relationship with Him was a free gift to begin with. His Holy Spirit even gave me the little bit of faith I needed when I asked Jesus into my heart. Planning our own destinies, being self-reliant, and watching out for ourselves-these things were at war in my mind with the things I was learning about my relationship with Christ. The Lord knows the future as well as my innermost being;

therefore, He knows what direction in life is best for me. I learned as I grew to know Him more, I would grow to know myself more. As a result I would better understand what my strengths are in relation to my future. He knows our hearts.

I also learned Christ does not want for us to go through this life alone. He wants to be a part of our everyday lives. Not just the trials and disasters, but the everyday and simple, to the good times as well. That is what a relationship with Christ is. He says come onto me all you that are heavy laden and burdened and I will give you rest. He wants us to come to Him. He wants to show us He is who he says He is. Try Him and see for yourself that He is the person He claims to be.

God clarified the reality of being able to have an actual relationship with Him during this time in my life. I seriously doubted whether or not Christ was speaking to my heart word for word or if it were in my head. I know a lot of people would say it was in my mind, or my conscience talking to me and I was mistaking it to be the voice of God. After all, why would the Creator of the Universe take the time to talk directly to a poor ex -gang member? I finally went to prayer and told Jesus Christ how I was having a hard time with this.

I heard that same peaceful-still small voice speak to my heart telling me to call Reverend Daniel. I hesitantly called. Gina, Reverend Daniel's wife, answered the phone. I asked to speak to Reverend Daniel; she said he wasn't there. Gina asked if there was anything she could help me with. I didn't tell her what I was bothered about, I asked her to pray for me, nothing more. Her prayer was the answer I needed. I remember it like it was yesterday. Gina prayed this prayer: "Lord I thank you for Ron, and I thank you that you are not a part of our imagination...Amen" I don't remember the rest of the prayer, all I knew is the first part of the prayer was all I needed to hear. The Lord spoke to Gina's heart showing her exactly what I needed to hear. He is real and He is near to those who seek Him.

The biggest miracle Jesus performed during this time in my life is something I will never forget for the rest of my life. I was in my car spending time alone in prayer and praise. The sun was starting to set. I was parked in front of my grandmother's house. It was raining lightly so I decided I would park the car under my grandmother's carport. Her carport was opened on three sides and had thick metal sheeting for a roof. A tin roof is what it is called. I could hear the raindrops hitting the metal tin roof.

After singing praise and worship, I felt the presence of the Lord fill the car. Then in the silence Jesus spoke to my heart. He spoke to my heart as a father would speak to his son, in an upbeat manner. He said, "Would you like to see me make it rain harder?" I responded to the Lord how He didn't have to do so to make me believe in Him any more than I already did. Then the Lord replied, "I know, but would you like to see me make it rain harder?" I said, "yes Lord, make it rain harder." Just then the rain picked up. I could hear the rain on the tin roof of the carport. I thought, "could this have been the Lord or is it my imagination?" I got excited believing it to be the Lord. What happened next erased any doubt that a miracle was taking place.

Jesus Christ spoke to my heart once more, "would you like to see me make it rain even harder?" I replied, "yes Lord, make it rain even harder." The rain instantly picked up and began to pour heavily. Again, I could hear it hitting the tin roof. Jesus spoke to my heart once again, "would you like to see me make it rain super hard?" Excitedly and with a giant smile on my face I said, "yes Lord, make it rain super hard." With that the rain turned fierce. It was coming down so hard and fast, the sound of it hitting the tin roof was so loud it hurt my ears.

Finally, Jesus spoke to my heart in a gentle, still small voice, "would you like to see me make it rain soft again?" With a complete peace in my heart, in a soft tone I replied, "yes Lord, make it rain soft again." Instantly the rain went from an ear-pounding storm to a soft sprinkle. Instantly. His peace filled my heart and my mouth was filled with praise. A scripture in the Bible talks about how Jesus calmed the storm for His disciples in the midst of a life threatening storm. Mark chapter 4, verses 39-41 reads: "And Jesus arose, and rebuked the wind, and said unto the sea, 'Peace, be still'. And the wind ceased and there was great calm. Jesus said to His disciples, 'Why are you so afraid? Do you still have no faith?' They (the disciples) were terrified and asked each other, 'Who is this? Even the wind and the waves obey Him!'" Prayer and praise from the heart allow us to hear God as he speaks to our hearts; prayer and praise from the heart invites God into the midst of our lives, to include our hurts, and misunderstandings.

There have been many times both as a youth and to this day as an adult I have felt I could bear no more. The Bible states that Jesus won't allow us to go through more than we can handle. The same Jesus, who calmed the storm for His disciple's centuries ago, is the same Jesus who will meet us in the midst of our storm, as we trust in Him to see us through. God speaks peace to our hearts as we praise Him. Prayers are answered. Miracles take place. His peace helps me to understand within the most inner part of my being, even when I don't have all of the answers. It is then that I know everything is going to work out for the good.

God gave me the inner strength I needed to press on in my faith, to do well in college, and to do well at work. In fact, I obtained a full time job with a major publisher as a graphic artist. The company offered a decent starting wage and full medical benefits. I was able to get my own apartment as well. My life was in direct contrast to the life my older brother Bobby was living. With the Earth Angels gang no longer around as an organized gang, Bobby, a.k.a. Huero, was now a full-fledged assassin for the Mexican Mafia. It was at about this time everything came crashing in on Bobby in relation to his involvement with the Mexican Mafia.

R.K. Jensen

BLOOD BETRAYAL

It turned out our dad was right about the Mexican Mafia using Bobby. Bobby was promised a lot and given nothing in return. He realized that after he lived out his usefulness as an assassin for the Mafia, the Mafia would then turn around and assassinate him. After he realized he was being used and going nowhere in the ranks, he decided he would send a message to the leaders of the Mexican Mafia, a message they could not ignore.

Bob, as mentioned, was the Sergeant of Arms for the Mexican Mafia. He was responsible for keeping track of all the weapons within the prison system such as zip guns, shanks, and razor sharp stabbing tools. In response to being used, he contacted a clean guard; a guard that was unsympathetic to the Mafia. He had the guard come to his cell. When the guard came he handed over to the guard all the weapons the Mafia issued to him. All the guns and all the shanks they had worked so hard to sneak in the prison system. Talk about a death wish. In the mob world you don't walk away and quit. If you do you will be killed. He wanted to send a message. They definitely got the message.

The Mexican Mafia quickly put out a contract on Bobby's life. They put another assassin to work and set a plan in motion. They would have to take Bobby by surprise. There was no one who could take him down face to face. The plan was put into play sometime later while Bob and all the other inmates were on recreation time in the prison courtyard. Bob was doing his regular routine of lifting weights. While he was lifting weights the Mexican Mafia caused a riot with another gang. The riot was a diversion. They had planted their assassin nearby Bob, moments before the riot broke out. The assassin waited in hiding with a shank and was ready to carry out the contract against Bob and at the same time score some major points with the Mafia's leadership. He was pumped and ready to go. As soon as the riot started and the guards did what the Mafia wanted them to do the assassin took out his shank and stabbed Bob repeatedly in the neck and head. Bob was bleeding badly. The riot ended and Bob was left lying on the bench press to die.

Just as my brother had told me, he was as good as and better at being an assassin than the Mafia leadership had feared. After the riot Bob was immediately taken to the prison hospital where he would eventually fully recover. He later told me personally that sometime after the stabbing he hatched a plan to get revenge on his attacker and on those who sent the assassin. Bob managed to get out of his cell and viscously attack the guy who had tried to kill him. Later, Bob ruthlessly carried out the assassination of a couple of the Mexican Mafia's main leaders to send a serious message to the top. They got the message and left him alone.

News got home about the contract and attempted hit on Bob's life. Helen was scared. I had never seen her so scared. We knew what gang life was like and the violence associated with it. But it wasn't as ruthless or as serious as violence associated with the Mafia. I asked her why she was so terrified. She told me something that frightened me. She said when the Mafia has a contract out on your life they sometimes go so far as to kill your family members to get to you. So inadvertently, Bob brought trouble on our entire family by joining the Mexican Mafia and then quitting the way he did. I was scared and at the same time upset with Bob for bringing this trouble on our family. I felt like I was in a mob movie, like a bad nightmare you can't wake up from, only it was for real.

By this time I moved into a larger apartment. I was working for the advertising agency as a computer graphic artist and going to college at the same time. I was still involved in Church as an assistant Youth Pastor. After recovering from his wounds, Bobby was released from prison. Bob eventually got married and had kids. He and his wife Betty lived a few blocks from my apartment complex. Betty was the younger sister of one of the former Earth Angel's gang members. She was now going to church. Whenever Bob and Betty needed some help I was there. Whether it was buying them dinner because they didn't budget their money, or teaching them how to plan a budget so they wouldn't run out of money, I was there to pray with them and help them make the transition from a life of drugs and the Mafia to a sense of normal living. Betty wanted to get involved in church. Although Bob was no longer in the Mafia or in a gang, he still spent time with old friends and family members that were still partying and getting drunk.

I learned from Mafia members the mob doesn't always carry out a contract to kill right away. Sometimes they will wait months, or even years if need be. The Mafia couldn't get near my brother, yet at the same time had not given up. They needed someone who could get close to him without his suspecting anything. They waited to find a way to get to him. Finally, years later they found a sure way of getting to him from his most trusted inner circle, they found a Mexican Mafia member named Anthony. Anthony had been a hardcore gang member in the South Bay area of Southern California. Here is the twist; Anthony's mother is my mother's sister. Anthony is our first cousin on our mom's side of the family. We knew his mom as this nice aunt we would go visit as children. His mom was married to a Dockworker, who worked the docks in Long Beach, California. Anthony was a gang member back when we were small children.

As it turned out Anthony did some things to get into trouble with the leaders of the Mexican Mafia. He knew they were going to seriously injure him, and more than likely were planning on killing him for messing up. The leadership knew Bobby and Anthony were cousins. The Mafia finally caught up with Anthony and told him if he did them a favor they would forgive him of his debt and let him live. They laid out the plan to him: get close to your cousin Bobby and carry out the contract as the assassin. In other words, kill Bob. Anthony accepted the deal and the Mafia had their inside man.

Anthony came down to our part of town and started hanging with Helen and Bob. He also spent time with other relatives in the area. They would party together, drinking and smoking pot. Helen said Anthony would give Bob hard looks the whole time. Nobody could figure out why. Bob didn't trust him, telling Helen and the others to be careful around him. Something didn't sit right with Bob. Yet no one could have ever expected what Anthony was planning.

Based on what I have learned about assassins and how they operate, Anthony was not chosen for being a well-trained hit man. He was only chosen because he was the only one who could strike from the inside, by betraying his own blood. On one particular Saturday, in the early evening when it was still light out, Anthony came to our neighborhood looking for Bob, without knowing exactly where Bob lived. He decided it would be a good idea to knock on different Apartment doors and ask if anyone knew Bob and where he lived. After finding Bob's apartment he simply knocked on the front door.

Bob answered the door with his little three-year-old girl standing directly behind him. Betty was in the kitchen cooking dinner. Without warning Anthony stuck a hand gun through the open door; Bob immediately threw his daughter to the side of the room onto the floor. Bob turned to run as he yelled to his wife Betty, "he's got a gun", warning her to hit the ground as Anthony pulled the trigger of the handgun several times. Loud shots rang out, bullets hit Bob once in the arm and the other bullet hit him right in the middle of the back, severing his spinal cord in half. A couple of bullets narrowly missed his daughter, and lodged in the wall. Anthony and an accomplice took off running down the street in broad daylight, in front of many witnesses.

My phone rang. It was Betty on the phone. She was frantic. "Bob's been shot, Bob's been shot. Come over quick." I ran over as fast as I could. When I got there two undercover cops were there with their guns drawn. Bob was on his way to the Hospital. The two undercover cops happened to be across the street purchasing drugs from a drug house when they heard the gunshots. It all happened so fast. The cops told me what had taken place after they talked to nearby witnesses, as well as to Betty.

Betty and her little girl were unharmed. Bob was flown to Loma Linda Medical Center. He survived his wounds, yet Bob was now paralyzed from the waist down. While he was in the hospital at Loma Linda Medical Center our dad Blade came out from the East Coast. Only this wasn't a friendly family visit. He came out on official mob business to end the contract on Bob's life once and for all, putting his own life on the line in doing so. He met with the Mexican Mafia's President and other leaders. His deal between the Arian Brotherhood and the Mexican Mafia was that they call off the contract on Bobby in return for higher-grade cocaine contacts. Blade was authorized by his mob group to offer the better source. They agreed but not without giving Blade a warning. They said if Bobby messed up again, not only would they kill Bob, but they would track down and kill Blade as well.

Right after making the deal Blade came over to my apartment. It had been many years since I had seen him. I wanted to show him how well I was doing. I showed him all the artwork I was doing in College and showed him samples of my work at the advertising company. He was anxious, very nervous, and in a hurry to go. He told me about the deal he had just made with the Mafia. He thought their members were following him. He also told me for the first time he was proud of me, although, it didn't carry much weight in light of the circumstances surrounding Bob's shooting. He said he needed to get out of town ASAP. I had never seen him shaken before. He was always so well composed and rough on the outside. The whole thing shook me inside. He didn't stay long and finally left.

The cops didn't find Anthony until about a week or

two after the shooting. He turned to some other relatives in our family asking for help. Our entire family was upset with him for betraying his own blood. His mom couldn't apologize enough, as she felt so bad for what happened. No one blamed her in any way. When Anthony showed up to get the help he needed the police were hiding out. When they knew for sure it was Anthony they arrested him. To this day he is serving two consecutive life sentences in prison.

Sometime after Bob recovered from his wounds his life fell to pieces. He completely lost his faith and once again returned to the street life as a drug user and alcoholic who hung around gang types. He and Betty separated. Betty kept the children while Bob moved back in with our mother. He went in and out of convalescent hospitals as well as the county jail. He continued to hang around the same old crowd. He slipped into a period of insanity for a short period of time. Even in a wheel chair he was a danger. Any time the cops found him out on the street they'd lock him up. They said he was a danger to himself. In the end Bobby lost his family, along with any hope of ever becoming someone with purpose and knowing the satisfaction of having accomplished anything in life.

My brother Bob had the same opportunities presented to him as I had. He could have stuck it out and would have come out all right, despite the many obstacles and trials we both faced. Instead, he chose a path of destruction. He had fifteen years of opportunity after opportunity to turn his life around. At one time a business-man of faith recognized how talented of an artist Bob was and offered to pay his way through graphic arts college once he completed the group home he was in. He joined Teen Challenge only to blow his chance at art school when he made the decision to walk away from the program before completion. Most of the men who complete the Teen Challenge program are able to maintain their sobriety and lead normal lives. God was there for him at every turn with open arms, desiring to set Bob free from a life of pain and hopelessness. I openly share with you that it truly saddens me as his younger brother how things turned out so badly for him in his life. I only wish I were making these things up.

  As I have learned through working with many inner city youth, you can only help those who truly want to help themselves. A special note to anyone involved in, thinking of becoming involved in, or you are trying to come out of drugs, gangs, and the mob. Please understand my brother received all that a life of gangs and the Mafia could offer, the only true guarantee the mob can make, and that is a life filled with no purpose, hard prison time, even at a young age, tremendous guilt, physically and mentally being paralyzed and or wounded, and now the possibility of dying at a young age from the bullet wounds. As the famous Mexican actor Antonio Benderras asks repeatedly in the newly released movie, *Once Upon a Time in Mexico*, I ask you, "What do you want out of life?"

ಸಿ R.K. Jensen ಲ

HIGHER GROUND

    Between church, school, and work I was extremely busy. I was working the late shift for the advertising company as a computer graphic artist. I'd leave straight from work to go to the College. When I wasn't sleeping I was doing homework. My friends told me I wasn't just burning the candle at both ends; I threw the whole thing into the fire. I was determined never to go back to a life of drugs, violence, and gangs.
    Anne, the pretty young lady I met in the Youth Group at church was now in charge of the youth group bulletin for the youth group. We were good friends for some time. About a year or so later she gave me a call and we got together for coffee. It was nice to hear from her. We started meeting for coffee and talking on the phone for hours at a time. Finally, I asked her out on a date to Disneyland. We spent the whole day talking and going on rides. By the end of the date I was head over heels in love with Anne and knew I wanted to spend the rest of my life with her. We started dating shortly thereafter. In getting to know Anne, I felt like I had always known her. She felt the same way. I was doing well at my job, so I took the opportunity to pay the balance on Anne's truck off. We were both quite happy with each other. The person in me she came to know is the person I became after the transformation in my life. She grew up in an affluent home in Glendora, California. She was attending college at the Pacific Design Center in Los Angeles, with a major in Interior Design.
    After dating for some time I decided I would ask

for her hand in marriage. I took her to a nice restaurant that sat on the edge of a cliff in Laguna Beach, California. The cliff overlooked the Pacific Ocean. The Palm trees swayed in the wind. As the sun set, coloring the blue sky a beautiful hue of reddish gold, you could see the silhouette of Catalina Island on the horizon of the Pacific Ocean. I knew it was the perfect moment, so I got down on one knee, pulled out the engagement ring and asked if she would marry me. She said yes as the other guests clapped.

 Anne and I were married in a beautiful historic church in San Dimas, California on July eighth, nineteen-eighty-nine. The back of the church was made up of a majestic pipe organ. All of the windows of the church were made of stained glass. The pipe organ rumbled as the wedding march was played. You could feel the vibrations of the pipes throughout the church. Anne came down the isle, with her dad at her side. I had never seen such a beautiful sight. Everything about that day was wonderful. It was truly one of the best days of my life. After the wedding reception we were off on our Honeymoon to beautiful San Diego.

 We moved to a new apartment complex in Upland, California. With what little savings I had left over after paying for the apartment and the honeymoon I bought some decent furniture for our new home. We had humble beginnings. That was all right because we had each other and in the center of our relationship we had our faith in Jesus Christ. We knew things would get better over time.

 About two months later she started getting sick in the mornings. She went to the Doctors and it turned out she was exactly two months pregnant. She became pregnant on our honeymoon. Despite what anyone thought about it, we knew this child was from the Lord and was on the way according to God's providential timing. Like anyone else, we had wanted to wait several years before we had our first child. The pregnancy was difficult. I was unable to attend classes at the College. The Doctor ordered Anne to bed rest. Anne was sick and couldn't hold down food. I was afraid for her. I thought she might lose the baby or end up in the hospital. I was able to get switched to the day shift at work and would call Anne during my breaks.

We had wanted to do a lot in our first year or two of marriage, have a good time, and grow close together. It was hard because I had to put my needs to the side and help her with her needs. She was understandably unable to take care of my needs. I eventually learned to put my needs to the side and be there for her. Through it I learned about a much deeper kind of love than I had ever experienced before. Love became something more than what I said to her. It became something I did. As a result I learned love is an action word; something you do regardless of how you feel at the time. We grew closer and our love for each other became stronger.

February 14th, 1990, Valentines Day came along and we had a special dinner. Soon after dinner Anne started having contractions. I timed them thinking it must be a false alarm. After all she was only seven months pregnant. After timing them for about thirty minutes, we realized she was in labor. We had only taken one out of four or five of the birth classes we were to attend.

We drove to Pomona Valley Hospital. They hooked Anne up to the monitors and then sometime later took her into the delivery room. So on Valentines Day, 1990 our son was born. We named him after myself. He was so tiny.

He was what they called a preemie, or, prematurely born. They let Anne briefly hold him then they whisked him away for test after test. This didn't seem like the typical delivery. The nurse came in and asked Anne many questions. We asked if something was wrong with our son. We weren't given any answers. I stayed by Anne's side as she slept.

The next day the Doctor came in to explain to us our son had problems from being born pre-mature. He said he had to be kept in an infant incubator. We were allowed to see him through the openings of the incubator. The Doctor later came back to tell us the hospital wasn't equipped to deal with our son's condition. He said our son would have to be transported by Ambulance to the Neonatal ward at Loma Linda University Hospital for specialized treatment. I held Anne. I called my Christian family and asked them to pray.

It came time for our son to be transferred to the University Hospital. They allowed us to spend time with him before he left. Wanting so badly to hold him and love him. All we could do was put our hands through an opening on the side of the little incubator. It came time for his departure. We felt as though he were being torn away from us. He needed his mommy and daddy. There was nothing we could do but pray.

As soon as Anne was discharged from the hospital we made our way to the University Hospital. I had a few days off from work. My co-workers were quite concerned as well. I told them I would keep them informed. We were at the hospital day and night. We even slept in the waiting room. The first time we saw our son he immediately responded to our voices and to our touch by kicking his legs and moving his arms around. The poor little guy was being fed through a tube. The veins in his arms were too small for an IV needle, so they had to put the IV needle in through a vein in his forehead. He had monitor wires and IV lines all over the place. It broke our hearts to see him in such discomfort. Especially when they took blood work for tests. I wanted to take his place and take all of those horrible tests for him.

Before we could see him we would have to scrub up and disinfect our arms and hands. When we did see him we were only able to put our arms through the holes in the incubator. Everything inside of me wanted so much to hold him. I would rub his bare back with my hand, call him by his name and tell him how much I loved him. This seemed to calm him.

After about a month he was moved from the fully encased incubator to an incubator that was completely opened on top. We were finally able to hold him. Anne and I would take turns holding him in a rocking chair next to his incubator. Although, not without all of his tubes and monitor lines. We felt a lot closer to him. By this time he would get excited when we came into the room. Our son knew who his mommy and daddy were.   I took a picture of Anne smiling as she held our son. We have this picture framed and placed on a mantle to this day.

After running days of tests the Neonatal Specialists called us in. We were told our son had some abnormalities. He had all of his hands, feet, fingers and toes. Internally, however, there were problems. It turned out he had two holes in the dividing wall of his heart, called the pericardium. His intestines were not connected at one point so he was unable to digest his food. They said they needed our consent to operate immediately on his intestinal tract.

They wanted to go in and close the holes in his heart as well, although the Heart Surgeon felt he was too young to survive the operation. We were told after his heart had developed more they would then operate on his heart. One of the Doctors was a little too forward. He said our son's chances of surviving either condition were highly unlikely. This hit Anne and me like a ton of bricks. The other Doctors brushed him off and said they felt good about his chances. First we would worry about the digestive problem.

  It came time to operate. He was out cold. He had his little arms and feet strapped out toward his sides. All I could do was hold Anne. We waited in the waiting room with relatives. We prayed that the little guy would survive the operation. Now all we could do was wait. The silence seemed to go on forever. I couldn't get myself to read a magazine or any thing else for that matter. My stomach was in knots. Finally the Doctor came into the waiting room. He told us our son had made it out fine. The operation to connect his intestines had been successful. There was hope he would soon be able to come home.

  At home we had a room all made up for him. Several of our friends and family had given us nice gifts for our son. Anne's dad bought a beautiful white furniture set that included a crib, changing table, and a cute bassinet. We received comforters with baby teddy bears. His room was all ready for him to come home to.

  The Neonatal nurse was an angel sent from heaven. Her name was Mary. The nurses try not to grow too attached to the babies. Mary, however, took a special interest in our son. She was nice to us and was a real support. She told us some of the premature babies never got a visit from their parents. That was the saddest thing I had ever heard.

Mary also showed us a collection of pictures that covered a wall in the ward. They were "before and after" pictures of premature babies who had come into the hospital and then went home with their mom's and dad's. They were so tiny at first, then to see them six months to a year later. It was incredible. Mary told us of a pair of twins who were both born under three pounds each. They didn't think the babies would make it. However, the twin's pictures were on the wall; beautiful little babies at home with their parents now happy and healthy toddlers. This gave us a lot of hope. It also served to show me the facts that those who choose to believe unborn babies in the womb are not fully human are not being honest with themselves.

 Our son began taking fluids into his stomach. He couldn't seem to get enough. He was able to digest his food. Anne gave me the honors of changing his first diaper. Wasn't that sweet of her? He started to grow and he became more alert. We could hold him and his eyes would fix on our eyes. He had such a peace about him. So much so he calmed my spirit. Several churches and ministries continued to pray for him. Over two months had already gone by. We were looking forward to bringing him home.

 During this difficult time in our lives, we were moved to pray for a family who had a young child in the Pediatric Cardiology ward for children with severe heart problems. This ward is where our son would need to go for his heart operation. Some of the children admitted there were waiting for heart donors. It is so hard to sit with your child when your child's life is at death's door. Not knowing whether or not this precious child will make it to the next day. This poor family was hit with a double tragedy. The child's father left the hospital with their older son to run down the street to the corner store. While driving he was in a fatal accident, a drunk driver hit him. The ambulance brought both him and his son back to Loma Linda where they both died. All we could do was to pray for this woman and her child.

We met one of the mothers whose daughter was in the Pediatric Cardiology ward waiting for a heart transplant. She was a Christian as well. She was holding up so well. She was a real encouragement to both Anne and me. Her daughter's heart transplant went well and after sometime in the hospital, she was able to go home. Her daughter was such a beautiful little girl.

Anne and I were attending a little church in Upland at the base of the San Bernardino Mountains. A young family at our church suffered a terrible tragedy as well. This young man was near completion of his college degree. His wife was expecting a child and they had a little boy as well. He was coming home from a family dinner when a drunk driver hit his car. He and their son were in the car and both died. Our church was there for both of our families. It seemed wherever we turned there was terrible heartache and pain in other peoples lives. The trials they faced seemed so overwhelming and unbearable, especially since we were facing a tragedy of our own.

The last word from Mary, the nurse who had befriended our family, was that our son was making great progress and we should be able to bring him home soon. He was growing so fast. Anne and I were feeling a lot better. Our hopes were up. My thoughts turned to the baby's room at home; we couldn't wait for him to come home.

At work they had been supportive and understanding. I came back from my extended leave. I think I only took an extra week off. About a month after I came back our supervisor quit to be closer to her son, deciding that time away from her son was not worth the price of having a career. The new supervisor had little experience in the advertising field. I was worried she wouldn't be as supportive about my family situation. As soon as work was over, or on the weekends, I would head over to the hospital to join Anne and the baby.

Our son had been in the hospital for two and a half months by this time. We were able to see him and hold him. One evening he felt a little cold. So I mentioned it to the nurse who was watching over him. She looked up from her book and nodded, then covered him up. After telling our baby how much we loved him we left. I went to work in pretty good spirits that next morning. Around noon I got a call from Anne. She was crying. I had to wait for her to calm down. She said Mary from Loma Linda called telling her to get there as soon as possible. Mary said our baby went into cardiac arrest and the emergency crew was working on getting his heart back. We were all crying. I told Anne not to drive by herself. I didn't want for her to risk an accident because of how upset she was. My supervisor said to go and off I went.

I picked up Anne and immediately headed for the hospital. On the way there I looked up at the clouds and saw them open. At that instant Jesus spoke to my heart and told me He had taken our son home. My heart was filled with a total peace. Anne told me the Lord said the same to her, she knew in her heart he had gone home to be with God. Our son received the ultimate healing. No more pain, no more crying, and no more tears. He was in the sweet arms of Jesus. Baby Keith went from the cold hospital neonatal ward to the warm and peaceful nursery in heaven.

As soon as we arrived at the Neonatal ward of the hospital, Mary met us and told us with tears streaming down her cheeks that our son Ronnie Keith didn't make it, he had not survived the ordeal and had passed away. Mary took us to a private room to console us. Anne and I were both somber and sad, yet at the same time I reassured Mary that our son was now in a much better place. Mary was an encouragement to Anne and me, and yet at the same time Mary was encouraged by the peace that Anne and I had. Anne later cried saying she had wanted to be there for him before he passed on. Baby Keith knew us as mommy and daddy. There was no doubt about that. Mary told Anne it was better we weren't there because we wouldn't have been allowed to see him while they were working on him. She said it was very traumatic. Baby Keith had a very nice stuffed bear that was big and very cute. We asked Mary to keep it because our son had meant so much to her. We were glad to know that during the times we were unable to be there she would give him extra care. Mary was touched and kept the bear.

The Pediatric Cardiologist told us because our son had been born with a heart defect that his heart was unable to keep up with the rate of growth his body had experienced. He wanted to do an autopsy to find out exactly why. We felt his little body had gone through enough already. We wanted to let him rest in peace.

At the funeral my Mom, my sister Helen, and my brother Jeff showed up. My Aunt Ricky and my Uncle

Eddie came to offer their support; it did my heart good to see them. My Aunt Ricky had helped raise me as an infant, and was their for me when I was in College. The majority of my wife's family came to support us as well. Many Christian friends came from all over. The support from everyone was encouraging to Anne and me. The line of cars seemed to go on forever. We buried our son on top of a hill near a lone tree. The memorial service was held at a little mountain church in Upland. The dinner was held at Jim and Malahli's home. When our son first passed away Jim was one of the first people I called, he cried with me on the phone. My Christian brothers and sisters had truly been a family to me.

  Well meaning people would tell me I would never know why the Lord took our son home. I know this is the best way they knew how to encourage us. Most others stayed away, not knowing quite what to say. I couldn't accept the notion that his death was for nothing and that I would never understand. As I had hoped Jesus spoke to my heart telling me how our son had touched so many lives. His short life had brought several people closer to Christ by bringing thousands of Christians together in prayer, all within two and a half months of his short meaningful life. Some people live their entire lives without ever making a positive impact in the lives of others. I know for certain his nurse Mary was especially touched. She said he had a peaceful spirit about him. Most of all he touched our lives. He had such a supernatural peace about him. His mission in this life had been accomplished. He was so special. What's more, heaven has become so real to Anne and me. Heaven went from the intangible to the tangible; more than a belief. We have someone who we physically held in our arms to look forward to seeing in heaven.

    Anne and I needed time to grieve the loss of our son. We knew in our hearts he was in a better place, yet it was difficult not having him at home to hold and care for. As a result I felt It necessary to take the weekends to be with my wife. Business was booming for the advertising company I worked for so the artists were being required to work overtime each and every weekend. I didn't mind working the overtime because it meant more pay, however, in light of our recent loss I was unable to work the overtime, which I explained to my manager.

    After the second week of not working the required overtime I was called into the office. The new supervisor lied and came up with some made up charges of insubordination not related to the overtime issue. I was fired. Judging by the woman's attitude on the phone at the unemployment office I knew I was made out to be the bad employee. The lies kept me from receiving any unemployment benefits. I went to the head of the Personnel Department at the advertising company trying to at the least get my job back. His reply totally floored me. He said to me, "I understand what you are going through. My dad died. And when he died I buried myself in my work." That was his answer. Bury myself in my work and forget I had a wife at home who was grieving for her son. All I could think was it was good for him and his wife it wasn't one of their kids who had died. I was out of a job without any prospects for a new one, in the early 1990's, the beginning of a major recession.

    We had a part time janitorial business. However, it wasn't enough to pay all the bills. I spent my free time looking for work. Some friends helped us out financially at times. Eventually I couldn't pay the rent on our apartment. I took a job as a waiter. I was so out of it my performance was lacking. I couldn't concentrate enough to remember what the orders were. I knew they needed my 100% and weren't getting it. The manager and I agreed I should leave the position. Sometime later I read that on an emotional level as hard as it is for a mother to lose a child, it is about as stressful on a man to lose a good job. So here Anne and I were going through the loss of my graphic arts job, our first-born son's death, and now our apartment. This was truly a dark time in our lives. This is the point where many couples choose to divorce, allowing bitterness and anger to set in and destroy what little is left of the relationship. To Anne and me our only choice was to run to Jesus in prayer in holding on to our faith and holding on to our relationship with each other. We started praying for miracles.

  Anne's mom let us stay in her condo until things got better. I finally found a job with another advertising company in Pomona. I worked the computer graphics station as well as developing the negatives for the press department. There were a lot of other new people there as well. This was in the early 1990's when the recession hit California and other parts of the country. Some of the new employees had been laid off from major corporations as a result of downsizing and from going out of business. We worked twelve-hour shifts. The first week I would work three twelve-hour days in a row, and the following week I would work four days in a row. I would work all the overtime I could.

  Anne was doing much better by this time. Although being out of regular employment for some time was hard, it allowed us to spend some much-needed time together.

A lot of healing, and growing closer together took place during this time. Anne's family even sent the two of us on a short vacation to San Diego. It was a nice rest. Her family was supportive during this time in our lives.

  Anne and I felt a void in our lives. Sure, we had the Lord, yet something was missing. We had a yearning to love and nourish a child. One cannot experience losing one's child without feeling this way. We realized our son could never be replaced. We decided to have another child. We prayed. Jim prayed for us as well. He said the Lord was going to bless us with a lot of kids. Anne was like, maybe not too many. Nine months later Anne gave birth to a healthy baby boy. We named him Seth. He was the calmest baby in the world, as well as the biggest. He weighed ten pounds when he was born. He started eating solids when he was only about two months old. Milk bottles wouldn't do. It was funny when he ate his bananas. He would gasp for air quickly in between bites. We couldn't feed him fast enough. Seth was truly a blessing from the Lord.

  We came to fully realize how much of a gift from the Lord Seth was when we looked up the meaning of his name in the Bible. We originally picked out his name only because we liked it. I knew at that time it was a Bible name, yet I wasn't exactly sure where in the Bible it was found. So one afternoon we sat down and looked through the Bible. I found the name Seth in the book of Genesis, chapter 4, verse 25. It says, "...and she (Eve) gave birth to a son, and named him Seth, for, she said," "God has appointed me another offspring in place of Abel..."" You see Eve had given birth to Seth sometime after her son Abel had died. We had no idea of the meaning of our son's name when we first named him. We felt so blessed to know Jesus cared enough about our needs and how we felt in that He had given us such a special blessing. Now we have a son we can love and raise in the Lord.

Anne and I decided we would start an educational program for inner city at-risk youth in California. Project Youth Challenge would teach at-risk youth work ethics, life skills, and Christian principles. My co-workers at work didn't think I could pull it off. Anne and I brought our talents together. Anne's fundraising and organizational skills, coupled with my graphics and youth ministry experience made for a good team.

I had several opportunities to share my life story with the youth. They enjoyed the program. Anne was working with the teens more so than I was. I was working at the advertising company, trying to build a career in the graphic arts industry. I was hoping to eventually land a position as an Art Director of an advertising firm. Good goals. However, the Lord had something much bigger and more important in mind.

I prayerfully made the decision to leave the advertising company to run Project Youth Challenge full time. Many lives would be touched and changed as a result of Christ using this program. Moreover, Anne and I were able to once again become financially stable, and move into a Town home with our newborn son. We were on a path of restoration. Our God is faithful to meet our needs and to restore what was taken away. Eternity truly is what matters most.

FORGIVENESS

On one particular Sunday, my wife Anne and I were visiting the Assembly of God church I had grown up in. Reverend Daniel and his wife Gina had moved on as Evangelists to the people of Armenia. Reverend Phil was now the Senior Reverend of the church. Reverend Phil was starting his sermon, when out of nowhere an older gang member burst through the back door of the church. He started raising his voice at the Reverend. Phil's assistant Paul motioned to escort this gang member out of the church. Phil said no, let him speak. I just about got out of my seat to confront this guy.

It turned out he was a guest speaker. He was speaking for a ministry that helped gang members. He had accepted Jesus Christ as a result of this ministry. He shared his story and then sang a nice song. Several youth responded to his message and gave their lives to Christ. This ex-gang member decided to join our church. His name was Manny. I had the opportunity to get to know Manny. It turned out the gang he was a part of in his past was the 12th Street Sharks. That really surprised me. So I thought to ask him what kind of car he drove back in the gang days, and he said it was a 1969 Chevy Impala. I thought, "This couldn't be". Could this have been one of my attackers when I was fourteen-years old? I was almost afraid to ask, yet I absolutely had to know. I asked Manny to describe his car. Manny said it was a gold-toned low rider and that it had a crack in the windshield. I was stunned and did not know what to say. I didn't know what to think. Manny was driving the carload of gang members that had shot and stabbed me when I was fourteen-years old. I immediately flashed back to the violent attack, I vividly remembered seeing the car pull up right in front of Snoop, Freddie, and me on that fateful night. I did not know how to respond. The Youth Minister of the church was standing nearby and motioned for a response. I put myself together and told Manny about the attack and how Jesus met me out in that field as I lay dying. I shared with Manny how I too gave my heart to Christ. I told Manny that I had forgiven him and his two accomplices a long time ago. In fact, I had prayed for his salvation and that of the other two gang members who were with him. I was finally able to put a face to one of my attackers. Here he stood a fellow believer in Jesus Christ sharing his testimony with our church about how Christ had changed his life.

We became friends after that. My brother Bob became his friend as well. I was a little worried about that at first, because the two at one time were bitter enemies, trying to kill each other during the gang wars. Everything turned out just fine. Manny told me about the guy they called Damon, the one who shot me multiple times. He said Damon was now paralyzed from the waist down. Damon's right arm was paralyzed as well. He made the comment that the injury of Damon's right arm was fitting since he had hurt so many innocent lives with that same hand. Manny also told me he was praying for Damon and has had opportunities to share his faith with Damon. I made it a point to pray for Damon. The Lord had blessed Manny with a good job and a modest home. God's perfect timing to bring people together, where healing and forgiveness takes place, is absolutely amazing.

Sometime later, Anne and I were on our way to

a major amusement park to celebrate our first wedding anniversary in July of 1990. I was so taken by our time together that I wasn't watching my speed. It didn't seem too fast. That is until I saw the red lights of the Highway Patrol car flashing in my review mirror. Of course, I had no one to blame but myself. The Officer came to my window as I was gathering together the forms I knew she would ask for. Just as she came to my window I overheard a call on her walkie-talkie. It was an urgent call. The Officer told me to watch my speed and that she would let me go this time because she had an important matter on her hands. Anne and I had a great time at the park and a wonderful first anniversary.

      The real miracle of this day wouldn't come to light until a few weeks later when I received a letter from a department store that stated I owed them a penalty fee of two hundred and fifty dollars for stealing from one of their stores on Valentines Day of that year. The letter went on to say that paying this fine in no way released me from any civil penalties that may have occurred as a result of my arrest for stealing. I was confused. I called this particular department store to find out what this was all about. They told me on February 14th, of 1990 I had been arrested for attempting to steal valentine's items from their store. I told the lady on the phone this wasn't possible and I didn't know whom they had arrested because on that particular day my wife and I were celebrating Valentines Day together and later that evening she went into labor. I was at the hospital with her, aiding her in the birth of our first son Ronnie Keith. Someone was caught stealing and then used my identity as their own. This person gave my full name, my social security number, and my driver's license number. She suggested I call the Chino Police department to see what was going on.

I called and to my shock there was an active warrant out for my arrest. Not for the person using my name, it was for me. I asked the officer on the phone what I should do and she told me all I could do was turn myself in and go to jail until it could be cleared up in court. How stupid is that? That was totally unacceptable. I had never been to prison and was not about to go. Especially for something I did not do. That was the miracle about my anniversary. I had no idea at the time I had an active warrant out for my arrest. When I didn't pay attention to my speed and got pulled over, the Lord in His divine timing worked it out to where this nice young Officer had to be pulled away at the exact moment she was going to write me up. Only she wouldn't have only written me up, she would have arrested me for the warrant when she pulled up my information on her computer.

I didn't turn myself in. I pictured the cops coming to my home to arrest me later that evening. The only thing I could think to do was to pray. So I went to my Heavenly Father and prayed. "Lord you know what is going on. You know I can't go to prison and have a prison record. I'll lose my job and become unable to find a new one. I don't know what to do or who to talk to. Please help me. Amen." The answer came as I waited on the Lord with an attitude of praise for His answer. In the quiet of the moment Jesus spoke to my heart and told me to call my wife's uncle Denny who himself is a Christian. I wasn't too sure how he could help but I figured it would be good to let him know what was going on so he could pray with me.

The Lord had much more in mind than Denny

praying with me. It turned out that Denny had years ago held a Bible Study in San Bernardino, which the Senior District Attorney of San Bernardino County had regularly attended. Denny told me his Christian friend the Senior District Attorney could help me with this case in Chino. So I gave the District Attorney's secretary a call and told her I was Denny's nephew and about my situation. The secretary took all of the information and told me that she would immediately give the details to the District Attorney. I thought for sure I would be put off and told to wait a week or two. However, I later got a call from the Chino Court and had a Court hearing scheduled for the very next morning. I was so surprised everything fell into place in one day. I didn't have to turn myself in.

After arriving to the Court House in Chino the next morning a Police Officer met me at the front desk and checked me for tattoo's that were a part of the identity of the person caught stealing. As mentioned, the person who gave the police all of my personal information also knew my driver's license number and my birth date. The tattoos listed were gang names, and a tattoo of an eagle, said to be a symbol of the Arian Brotherhood. I had none of those tattoos. After seeing the judge I was exonerated, or pardoned of all the charges. By the description of the person arrested, as well as the tattoos listed, I knew the person using my name was none other than my younger brother Jeff. We were about the same height, and we both had an olive complexion with black hair. The difference was that he looked and dressed like a gang member, and had a criminal record that was pages long. I was clean cut, I had no tattoos, and no criminal record as an adult. To top it all off, what really got me was he did it the day my son was born. As if going through the ordeal with my son weren't enough. I knew Satan was using him. The timing was too perfect to think it a coincidence.

  At Calvary Church, Anne and I helped form a young marriage group called Couples Alive. It seemed like a good name for the group at the time. We met a nice young couple named Jeremy and Carol. They had two boys named Tom and Jeremy Jr. We went on a lot of outings together and they would come over and go for a swim in our pool. We would see each of our families go through some pretty rough trials together. It was a blessing to know them, especially after having lost our son. Jeremy studied to become a Sheriff and did just that. He landed a job at the newest multi-million dollar correctional facility in Rancho Cucamonga. They nicknamed it Club Fed. Apparently it was state of the art. Not in respect to the type of security. More so in respect to the amenities provided to the inmates.

  One evening while fundraising with the teens in Project Youth Challenge I decided I would go to a nearby town that I was unfamiliar with. People unfamiliar with our program called the police on our teens. The police came out to see what was going on. The Officer told me he didn't mind our fundraising, yet he had to answer the call. He asked for my identification as a matter of routine. I was somewhat upset people would call the police on young teens trying to stay away from drugs, gangs, and violence. The officer turned to me and asked if I knew I had a warrant out for my arrest for drug possession. I was floored. I quickly explained to the officer about my younger brother Jeff. My thoughts were racing in my head at about a hundred miles a minute.   There are many people in the prison system as a result of somebody using their identities. I quickly thought to tell him about my brother's tattoos and that if he looked at the description of the person charged it should list his tattoos. He asked me to take off my shirt and show him my back. Embarrassed and in front of all the teens in Youth Challenge, I took off my shirt and showed the officer my back. My wife must have been praying inside of the van because the officer let me go. The teens thought it was the coolest thing in the world, it is all they talked about on the way home.

  It turned out that while Jeff was incarcerated in jail his wife was tossing narcotics through the back fence of the prison. He would later walk over to the site and pick up the drugs and use them while locked up. Whenever his wife went to go visit Jeff she said her name was my wife's name, Anne. His wife had to do this because Jeff was in jail under my name. The next time she visited Jeff the guards caught him with the drugs. His wife was prohibited from visiting Jeff. They released Jeff before they realized he was in there under the false pretense that he was me. He made a promise to appear in court for the drug charge. Of course, he did not show up. There was one other time that Jeff was locked up. He ended up at Jeremy's Club Fed. Jeremy asked me if I had a brother with the same name. I asked him why. He told me there was a guy in jail who looked like me with the same exact name. The next time he went back to work he asked Jeff if he had a brother named Ron. Jeff responded that he did. Jeremy told him he knew who he was. He said, "your not Ron, Jeff." Jeff freaked and said it wasn't true and then as Jeremy walked away Jeff kept yelling, "how did you know, how did you know." Jeff's plan was simple. I didn't have a police record of any kind as an adult. He had a rap sheet about as long as a novel. He got away with the stealing charge at the Department Store and figured he now had a clean slate with my clean record. No concern whatsoever as to what might happen to me.

I had to go to court twice on this new drug charge. I missed the first scheduled court date because I got the date mixed up. My life was moving fast and keeping up with what my brother was doing was taxing. Therefore, when I did get to the court the Judge laughed at me, saying I was probably lying to him about my brother. He didn't take me seriously, and he threatened to have me arrested if I forgot about the court date again. Jeff was out and about living a life of drugs and crime. I knew I had to clear my name before he messed it up any more with new crimes, or worse, I could end up in prison for a long time.

Jeremy was a Godsend. Jeremy wrote a letter to the court supporting my character that also stated how he had run into Jeff when Jeff was locked up in jail while using my name. The police put together a sting operation and went to Jeff's house where they arrested him without incident. When Jeff finally did go to court he denied the whole thing. Jeff told the court I was the one in jail during this time, saying I was the one getting the drugs while in jail. He blatantly lied, knowing full well I would have to go to jail in his place. I was told not to attend the trial unless Jeff wouldn't admit to the crime. Instead, I was given a number to call that went directly to the courtroom. Jeremy was there at the trial. Having Jeremy there helped turn things around. Jeff finally admitted to the drug charge and having maliciously used my name in the committing of crimes. I called the court and was told not to bother coming down.

I was once and for all exonerated of all charges. I received a full pardon. I was assured that he could no longer use my name to commit crimes because it was being noted in the central computer system. This had gone on for two years. It finally came to an end. I didn't have to spend one day in prison. Prison is something I feared and swore I would never go to. My dad, along with my brothers Bobby and Jeff, had been in and out of jail for years on end. I didn't want to suffer the same fate. As hard as it was to understand why Jeff would do such harmful acts toward me, and why my Mother and sisters would go along with it while they visited him in prison, I honestly felt sorry for Jeff. As hard as it is to believe, my own Mother played along with his stealing my identity, as did other family members that went to visit Jeff in jail. How could they not know that this could have ruined my entire life in every way. Still, my heart broke for Jeff in that the abandonment he suffered by our mom and his dad (we had different dads) left him with no support. He ended up stuck in strict poverty, he was illiterate, he suffered from disease, was imprisoned, and addicted to drugs. I would be lying if I didn't say I was hurt and upset at him for what took place. Yet I was moved to pray for Jeff and his wife, and with Christ's help, I completely forgave him. I forgave my Mom and my sisters as well.

Jeff served out his sentence for the drug charges and managed to stay out of trouble for some time. I don't know whether or not he joined the Arian Brotherhood, yet it wouldn't be long before he found himself tangled in a crime spree with the white mob, as he continued to slip into the way of the mobster.

RETURN OF THE MOB

Anne and I moved into our first single family home in 1992. It was a nice change from apartment living. Project Youth Challenge was in its second year and doing very well. Around this time I got the news from my family that my dad was in a hospital on the East Coast. No one knew exactly why, although it sounded pretty serious. The last time I saw or heard from my dad was when the Mafia shot Bobby about four years earlier. I called my dad, who as mentioned earlier goes by the alias Blade. I found out Blade was at the drug rehabilitation ward of the hospital. He was detoxifying from, or coming off of the regular use of the drug Heroin. He also had alcohol-induced cirrhosis of the liver that came from years of alcohol abuse.

Anne and I talked it over and decided I should attempt to get him enrolled in a Christian Men's Home here in California. I contacted a couple of the one's located in the area. Teen Challenge was full and had a long waiting list so that was out. A close friend of mine had gone through a Christian Men's Home nearby. My friend graduated from the program a changed man. My friend had a real positive outlook and hope for the future, he had found a relationship with Christ and new meaning to his life. My hope was that Blade would want to go through the program and find the same thing that my friend had, freedom from addiction and a new hope in Jesus Christ.

I got in touch with the director of this home. He said they would take my dad if he was willing to come and willingly submit himself to the program. I explained to him

Blade was detoxifying and he said that wasn't a problem. I spoke to Blade over the phone in the hospital. I was reluctant to ask him. To my surprise he said he would come out and go through the program. The airline reservations were made and within two weeks he would arrive at LAX International Airport. The plan was to come to California and go straight into the program.

I should have seen his arrival as a bad sign of some sort. The day the plane touched down in Los Angeles there was a severe rainstorm. Roads were flooded and the heavy rain made it difficult to see. I finally got off of the freeway and headed down the last stretch of road toward the airport. The road was flooded with several feet of water. Several stalled cars that had tried to pass through blocked the way. I was driving a one-ton van so I drove with one side of my van on the concrete Island in the middle of the road with the other side of my van immersed in water. I made it through.

I finally arrived at the airport a few minutes late. His plane had already touched down and unloaded the passengers. He was nowhere to be found. I waited by the baggage area figuring he would be gathering his bags off of the luggage carousel. I found his bags; they were the last ones on the carousel. Blade was nowhere in site. Finally, airport security came up to me and asked if I were Blade's son. I said I was, wondering if he had gotten sick on the plane or something. They took me to where the plane was. Next to the plane was an ambulance with its red and blue lights flashing. It turned out he was suffering from withdrawals. This is a symptom of coming off of a drug that a person has been addicted to for some time. The hospital hadn't given him enough medication to last

the trip.
 They carried him away on a stretcher and took him to the L.A. County General Hospital. I had such a bothered feeling inside I felt like turning back to go home; leaving him at the hospital. I couldn't understand the way I was feeling. I got directions to the hospital and shortly thereafter was on my way. I got to the hospital to find Blade in the emergency room. He was delirious. The staff couldn't get anything out of him. He kept saying the name of the medication he needed along with some profanities. Our reuniting after four years had been unpleasant to say the least. He was finally released the next morning. When he came out I could barely recognize him. I wondered if perhaps this were an entirely different person. He said, "What's the matter, aren't you going to give your old man a hug?" I reluctantly said yes and gave him a hug.
 Introducing Blade to Anne the next day was embarrassing. I didn't hate Blade or anything. It is just that when you introduce your parents to the one you love, namely your wife, you want it to be under better circumstances. Blade slept the entire first day or two at our home. It was late February or early March of 1993. I took Blade to the Home that week. The man who welcomed us into the office was a real tough guy. He looked at Blade and didn't seem to like him much. When the director came he introduced himself to Blade. The director was an ex-drug user himself. He had been in and out of prison for some time before coming to know the redeeming power of Christ. Then after years of knowing and serving the Lord started this men's home. The guy who first welcomed us started giving Blade a hard time. "You got to cut your hair and get rid of the cigarettes man." I thought this guy

needed to bug off. Finally, the director asked him to leave. He explained the rules to Blade and asked if he were ready.

  Blade told the director that he was still detoxifying. The director said they had no facilities for that and he could not join the program until after he detoxified. I explained to the director that I was told it wouldn't be a problem. He apologized and said it isn't a good idea. He did say Blade could try to detox cold turkey. In other words they would accept him in now; only he would have to finish detoxifying without any medications. I knew the Lord could see him through it. However, the director cautioned that he has seen men die from the withdrawal symptoms while trying to detox "cold turkey".

  I took Blade back home to my place. He decided he would rather stay with us while he detoxified under medication. Even with the medication he had been experiencing withdrawal symptoms. Anne and I discussed it and decided he could stay a couple of weeks while he detoxified. I thought it would be a great opportunity to share the Lord with him.

  After the two weeks had passed Blade asked Anne and I to come into the kitchen for a "family" meeting. He felt he no longer needed the men's home. He said he wanted to start over here in our hometown. He saw a mobile home nearby that he could rent with my brother Bobby. He asked if he could stay a while longer while putting this together. He also wanted to buy my extra van off of me so he could start a vending business. I was saddened that he didn't feel the need for the men's home any longer. That was the whole reason for his coming out. I felt bad for Anne because none of this was supposed to

happen. She wasn't too sure about it. So we talked and decided it would be all right for him to stay.
Things seemed to be going pretty smoothly. Blade was going by the rules we had laid down when he first arrived, with the exception of eating all the sweets in the house. One of the main rules was to have no contact with my family while staying in my house. For certain, if he got in touch with them he would easily end up back on drugs. Heroin was easily obtainable and some in my family were drug dealers and drug users.
While Blade was with us his 45th birthday came up. Anne and I decided we would have a surprise birthday party for him. I made reservations at a local favorite Victorian restaurant called the Spaghetti Factory. Anne and Seth were with me. I called Blade at home and told him my van had broken down and that I needed him to come and fix it. When he arrived at the restaurant we surprised him with a cake and a gift. He was pretty surprised and we all had a good time.
Anne and I had found a small Calvary Chapel church that bordered San Jacinto and Hemet. Blade finally agreed to go to service with our family. This was the first time our pastor preached the salvation message since we started going to the church. He went through it step by step. I knew the Lord was dealing with Blade's heart. Finally, the Pastor gave the invitation for any one who wanted to receive Christ as their personal Lord and Savior. Blade rejected Christ. He wanted nothing to do with a relationship with the Lord. My hopes were dashed to a thousand pieces. I knew in my heart this could be the last opportunity Blade could have to accept Christ. I prayed hard. Still, Blade didn't respond and said no. I

didn't know what to expect next. Anne and I were in no way prepared for what was about to take place. There is so much that happened I could write a book about what would take place in our lives over the next few weeks and months ahead.

It came time for our monthly trip for the youth in Youth Challenge. The teens had been working on a trip to Six Flags Magic Mountain. I figured Blade would go with us. The day we were to leave for the trip he said he didn't want to go. He said he'd rather stay home. Anne and I took off to pick up the teens. On the way we spotted Blade driving Anne's truck on the freeway headed in the same direction as we were headed. We caught up to Blade and pulled over to the side of the Interstate 10 Freeway. He told us that he had gotten lost while trying to find the detox center in Riverside. I pointed him in the right direction and off we went to Six Flags Magic Mountain with the teens.

When we got back late that evening Blade had some gifts for Seth. He bought him a large plastic racecar and some other things as well. He said he got the money from selling the rest of his supplies for his vending business. The only problem was there weren't many supplies left to sell. Later that week Anne took the money from inside our closet to go make money orders for supplies. She came back in tears. When she counted the money she found she was about eight hundred dollars short. She said that Blade had gone through our room while we were at Magic Mountain with the teens. I didn't want to believe he would steal from his own family. I asked Anne if she counted it right. She had. We looked all throughout the room and found nothing. Finally, I had to confront Blade. He flatly denied it. I told him he had to leave my home. To top it off, I found out while we were gone on the trip, he went and visited my family and bought them gifts as well. I also took the keys to the van he was buying from me. This was one of hardest things I ever had to do in my life. He went crazy. I took him down the street to a pay phone so my family could come and pick him up. I had to get his stuff together and drop it off to him at the pay phone.

I went through his suitcase. I found a set of scales that are used for weighing out drugs when selling drugs on the streets. I remembered coming home the day before and smelling a horrible smell coming out of the microwave. In the trash I found a burnt spoon. He had been using heroin in my home as well. All the dots started to connect. He was also processing the drugs in bulk for distribution. Little did I know the great evil he had been up to, or the evil that was about to take place.

I took his belongings to him while he was on the phone. It was cold and the wind was blowing. He said as I walked away that he did not take the money and he hoped I would find it. As I drove away I could see him standing there alone, with all he owned in the world sitting in one large cardboard box. I felt sick inside. I was torn between Anne and the man I thought to be my dad. I didn't want to believe he would do such a thing.

Blade came by a few times after that to pick up his disability check. On one particular day, my brother Jeff brought Blade by in his brown Toyota Celica. It was older and was missing a hubcap or two on the passenger's side. Blade came up to the door. I was so saddened by the site. He had open sores all over his face that were oozing with a clear fluid. He looked terrible. As I handed him his check, he could barely look me in the eyes. He finally looked up at me with tears in his eyes and said he was sorry. He didn't say what he was sorry for. I took it to mean he was sorry for the way things had turned out. However, I wondered if he were saying sorry for something he was about to do. He took off with Jeff. Jeff had some hard looking men in the back of his car. They all gave me hard looks as they drove away. I had never seen these men before. They were members of the white mob, the Arian Brotherhood.

Anne mentioned to me that after she sent out our bills the payments had never been received. Someone had taken the money orders being sent with our bills out of our mailbox. We started to get scared. Blade told us some pretty horrifying stories about his involvement with the mob while he was staying with us. Blade told stories that involved kidnapping children from parents who owed a bad drug debt and then selling them as slaves on the black market on the East Coast. How Blade had murdered and dissected a prostitute who was keeping money back from him for her prostitution money that she brought in each evening. One night our dog started barking. Our window was slightly opened and I thought I heard someone outside of Seth's window call out the dog's name. I brought the dog inside and then brought Seth into bed with Anne and me. It was pretty scary. I had no idea how evil Blade truly was.

Easter Sunday came and the tradition was for our family to go to Anne's Aunt's house for Easter. All of her family was gathering there for the holiday. Anne didn't want to go for fear that Blade might break into our house to steal. When we came home that evening our house had been broken into and ransacked. I asked the neighbors what they had seen. They saw a brown Celica parked nearby with Blade sitting inside. They saw Jeff walking back to his car with a stereo and a medium sized suitcase. They didn't think much of it at the time. I didn't want to involve them any more than that. They didn't need the trouble of the mob on their hands. Jeff had taken apart the window frame to my office. He took all of Anne's jewelry, Seth's whole piggy bank of around two hundred and fifty dollars, and the stereo. He looked in all the places where we kept the cash, which confirms that Blade took the money in the first place. Fortunately, we had made a bank deposit before Easter Sunday.

    We figured there was only one thing left to do. Move as far away from the area as we possibly could. After losing the money and some of our belongings, we didn't have the money on hand to make a big move. It was still pretty early in the month and I had already paid the rent. Anne and I stuck everything from inside of the house to inside of the garage. I reversed the lock on the garage door that led to the inside of the house so you could only get inside the garage through the side yard door. We talked to Anne's mom. It turned out that her husband had a vacant rental available. He didn't rent it to us; he generously let us stay in it while we saved up to make the big move. All we had in the empty house was about a week's worth of clothes for Anne, Seth and me, and a mattress with blankets and pillows. Everything else was locked in the garage back at the house. The lady who lived two doors down from me in San Jacinto offered to watch the house and to stay in contact with Anne's mom.

    I called every Christian I knew, asking them to pray for our safety and for the Lord's provisions. This had to be one of the darkest times of my life. I felt like I couldn't think straight for anything. Anne and I needed some things from the garage so we went back to pick them up. When we opened the garage we found that my dad and Jeff had indeed returned. They had lifted the side of the garage door and crawled underneath and then slid as much of our stuff as they could through the opening. Anne's guitar and our microwave were gone. A fan I used during the hot summer months was gone as well.

Finding these missing items was only the tip of the iceberg. I picked up the newspaper and gave it to Anne. She read the first page and gasped for air. She showed me the article in the paper. I was astounded at what I read. The bank in Hemet had been robbed a day or so before Easter. The robber wore a flannel shirt, glasses, and a baseball cap. The get-away car was described as a brown vehicle missing a hubcap or two on the passenger's side. Blade had stopped by my house with my brother in his brown Celica to pick up his check that exact same day. That was around noon. The bank was robbed about one to two hours later. Several other banks in the area had been robbed, including bank robberies in Riverside. Looking back I remember that sometime before Blade was asked to leave my home he had sent for that same flannel shirt, hat, and sunglasses from his wife on the East Coast. He had been planning to rob those banks all along.

From what I learned from the media and my family, Blade and Jeff would drive up to the bank at around 2:00pm, perhaps because there are fewer people in the bank during this hour. I would imagine that while Jeff and one of the accomplices waited in the car, Blade would enter the bank. Blade would patiently wait his turn in the teller line. When it was his turn, Blade would present himself as charming as can be, it is rather disarming, yet when he handed the teller the note demanding money and said he had a gun, he turned dead serious. He quickly and quietly took the money, left the building, jumped into Jeff's waiting car and drove to the Inland Empire where Jeff lived. The only problem was that a witness got a good look at Jeff's car and the surveillance cameras got a good image of Blade in his flannel, hat, and dark sunglasses.

As it turned out every first couple of days of the week Jeff and Blade would stop at the Post Office in Jeff's car to pick up Blades mail, near where he robbed the banks. This is how Blade got himself caught. The FBI had surveillance set up in the area for about a week. Blade also left a pattern to the Bank Robberies. All the banks he hit were in North East Riverside County. Once the FBI Agents became aware of a similar car coming to the Post Office in that area the FBI Agents set up a sting operation at the same post office where Blade picked up his mail in my brothers brown car.

The FBI hid out at the Post Office. The Post Office workers remembered what Blade looked like and would signal to the FBI when he arrived. The day finally came when Jeff and Blade pulled up in the brown Celica to the Post Office. Blade came to get his mail, unaware of what was waiting for him. As soon as the Post Office employee signaled the FBI, more than a dozen armed FBI agents swarmed in on him. They had Blade lying on the ground as they pointed their shotguns and handguns at his head. Jeff saw what was going on from outside and decided that he didn't want a part of it, deciding to leave Blade behind. As he started driving away he was surrounded by several patrol cars. Had he tried to make a run for it he would

have been shot and killed on the spot. He surrendered.
  Anne and I had finally saved enough money to move as far away from all of my family's troubles. This would be one of the biggest moves and one of the biggest acts of faith either one of us had ever taken. We were moving to an area where we pretty much didn't know any one. We had no ministry or church contacts. I would have to start our inner-city youth outreach program all over again. The road leaving California through the mountains and desert seemed so long and so quiet. All I could think about was moving my family to safety. We felt like a darker chapter in our lives was ending. We were embarking on a new and mysterious journey in our lives. I was thankful to God for delivering us. I was also thankful for Anne's mom who was truly an Angel during this difficult time. She and her husband unselfishly helped us out by allowing us to stay in one of their rentals in California prior to our big move. She was a real encouragement to Anne and me.
  Blade had a plan in place that if he got caught for the Bank robberies his mob buddies would pull a bank robbery in the same exact way he had, figuring that the F.B.I. would have to let them go. And that is exactly what they did. Blade is a career criminal and knew how to work the legal system to his advantage. The F.B.I. thought they had the wrong guys and consequently had to let Blade and my brother Jeff out of jail.
  After leaving jail Blade stayed with Jeff and his wife. While staying there Blade bought himself a late model Cadillac. What he did with the rest of the money was a mystery. My guess is that he spent it on drugs. He finally flew back to the east coast near New York, leaving the car with my mom. I was not in California when he was released

from jail, I only learned about all of this from an unnamed relative who Blade stayed with after being released from jail.

Blade was now gone for good. He had no plans to return to California or to contact me in any way that I am aware of. Because of his involvement with the mob this would be best for the safety of my family. I found out sometime later that after Jeff was released from prison he committed his life to Jesus Christ. I was told Jeff was very serious about his newfound faith. However, the years of drug and alcohol abuse to Jeff's body proved to be too much. At about twenty nine-years of age Jeff slipped into a coma. After two and a half months in the coma Jeff passed away. It turned out that Jeff had an inoperable cancerous brain tumor. God spared Jeff a lifetime of pain and took him to a peaceful place in heaven, a wonderful example of God's amazing grace.

Anne and I had some wonderful news during this time. Anne was pregnant with our third child; however, this was being overshadowed by the events that were taking place with my dad and brothers. I was worried she might miscarry from all of the stress of what we were going through. As a result of all the trouble my parents and brothers had caused us I wondered if Anne and the kids would be better off without me. She and the children certainly didn't deserve any of it. She deserved much better than having to flee our home. I had to wonder if reaching out to others, especially to Blade, was worth it. Was going through such pain worth serving Jesus? So many questions and so much hurt, we were both left wondering how the Lord could allow such a thing in our lives.

Anne and I talked and prayed about the whole situation. Anne assured me she did not blame me for what had happened in any way. We both had a lot of regrets about Blade, not about each other. She said in so many ways she would stay with me. She trusted in the Lord and knew He would see us through. We both knew we were meant for each other and that God has great plans for us. Not just plans for Youth Challenge, future plans for our new family as well. Still, that nagging question was in the back of our minds. How could the Lord allow us to go through such things when all we wanted to do was to serve Him?

Jesus our Lord didn't judge us or get angry with us for feeling hurt and let down. He loved us and covered us with His peace. He gave us the promise that He would personally restore what Satan had stolen away from us, such as the joy of our faith, our ministry working with youth, and feeling safe and secure in our home - with a healthy family, along with my good name and reputation. According to God's faithfulness and grace the answers to our prayers and questions did come, along with a complete restoration of our lives, over the next several months, and years ahead.

R.K. Jensen

PLANS FOR GOOD

Jeremiah 29:11 "For I know the plans that I have for you", declares the Lord, "plans to prosper you and not to harm you, plans to give you hope and a future."

Anne's dad set up our stay at a luxurious hotel in the city we moved to. We received the royal treatment at the Embassy Suites. I was grateful for his help, and thanked the Lord for a nice place to recuperate from the long drive. Anne obtained rental guides and the Sunday paper to find homes available for rent. As it turned out there were more people moving into the area than there were houses available. Whenever we pulled up to a home we would pull up along side two or three other families wanting to rent the same home. Together Anne and I sat on the couch in our hotel room and prayed. I didn't get a verbal answer, yet I received an inner peace. Sometimes that is all it takes to know the Lord is fully in control and about to perform a miracle.

We got a call from a manager of a town-home. He said he received a message we were looking for a place. He was nice on the phone and told us the town-home was new in a nice part of town near a beautiful lake. He said another couple was scheduled to meet him the next morning and if they didn't want it that it was ours to rent. We were scheduled to see it half an hour after the first couple. I brought a check with me ready to give it to the manager, hoping this was the answer to our prayers.

We got there and the manager took us on a tour of the town-home. It had a beautiful brick and stucco exterior, a fireplace, with three levels and plenty of storage, along with two large bedrooms, a large living area with a kitchen, a dining area, and a living room. It was the right price and was nicer than a lot of the homes we had looked at. After seeing it the manager asked if we liked it. We quickly responded yes. The town-home was ours. I later asked the manager why the other couple didn't show up. He said they had a flat tire on the way to see the town-home. They said they were pretty disappointed about it because they were planning on renting it. Anne and I were thankful for a much needed answer to prayer.

  I felt reassured we would do well with the youth program in our new hometown after talking to our fundraiser supplier in Southern California. It turned out we relocated to the exact area where our supplier had started out in youth ministry with a major church in the big city. He said he would pay the costs of setting up a warehouse for the fund raising items needed to support the program. Even though only a few teens showed up during the first week of the program, I conducted the program as though we had a full group. Eventually, the program grew to about fifty plus teens, along with other adult youth workers.

  My wife Anne gave birth to our third child in the winter of 1993. We had a baby girl. She was born healthy, and we named her Audrey. We could tell she was going to be tall because she was so long and skinny. Audrey was born with pretty blue eyes and very little hair. When we brought her home from the hospital, Seth, my two-year-old, thought we brought her home for him. His first reaction was to grab a book and attempt to read her a story. When I put her to bed Seth cried that he wanted her back. We were glad Audrey was born healthy. We were able to pay for the delivery with no problems. After living nearby the beautiful lake, Anne and I moved from the town-home and were finally able to buy our first home in a nice neighborhood.

In the new area Anne and I were living the economy was thriving, consequently about nine months later, we sold our first home and took the money to buy a much larger beautiful home that sat on close to an acre of land with a natural preserve on the property. The natural preserve looked like it must have looked when Indians lived on the land. It wasn't uncommon to see deer, or a den of foxes wandering through the property. Whenever it snowed, I would take the kids sledding down the hill in our back yard. I was blessed to see our young family growing and prospering.

I had lost all contact with my brother Bobby after I relocated my young family. With our cousin Anthony in prison and the contract called off on Bobby's life because of the deal Blade put together with the leaders of the Mexican Mafia, Bob no longer had to worry about a mob hit on his life. As mentioned, Bob's life fell to pieces after the shooting. Such as when his wife left him, and he suffered a brief period of insanity. After some time Bob finally broke off all ties with my entire family and disappeared without telling anyone where he was going. He knew that I had done the same and that it was necessary in order to never go back to the life of the mobster. Bob finally stopped taking drugs and regained his sanity. My family tracked Bobby down close to a year later and found that he had admitted himself into a convalescent home for the disabled. He also rededicated himself to his faith in Jesus Christ, and this time stayed true to the faith. From what I was told, while in the hospital Bob became ill. Bob had sores from sitting in his wheel chair too long. These sores went untreated for some time while he lived with our mother. Because of this and mostly because of his previous bullet wounds from when Anthony shot him, Bobby developed a fatal blood disease. While in the convalescent home Bobby fell into a coma and soon afterwards passed away, in a similar way our brother Jeff had passed away. With Bobby now dead, our cousin Anthony was retried in the courts for pre-meditated murder and was convicted on all counts. Anthony was sentenced to two consecutive life sentences. Anthony sits in a California prison to this day, as he will for the rest of his life. Even worse than the life sentence in prison Anthony received, is that the leaders of the Mexican Mafia decided to renew the contract on Anthony's life. I feel it is important to say that as hard as it is, I have completely forgiven Anthony for murdering Bobby, in the same way Jesus has forgiven me for my sins.

    I was saddened to have lost my brothers. I was hit particularly hard when I was told that Bobby died and I wasn't able to make the funeral. I was glad to hear that he rededicated himself to his faith in Jesus Christ, yet I was sad that I was not able to see him. The loss I had felt as a youth when Bobby left home to join the gangs was now compounded by his death. I now had no living full-blood relatives. I felt alone. I didn't have anyone to talk to about it that would understand. I tearfully went to the Lord in prayer and He comforted my heart. I caught a glimpse of Bobby in heaven, he was in his right mind, he was happy, and all his tattoos were gone. The wheel chair was gone as well, and he had a peaceful look on his face. I felt like God was showing me that Bobby was fully restored now, and that he would be waiting there for me when my turn comes to go to heaven. I was able to move on and concentrate on my new family and on the young teens that I was helping to stay away from drugs, gangs, and violence through the youth program Project Youth Challenge.

In our youth program we wanted to reach youth at the age where they are the most open and at the point of making decisions that impact the rest of their lives. The youth in this age range are more open to learning and applying the principles to overcome obstacles than older teens that have already made up their minds about the way they want to go. As a result of our efforts several young teens on their own initiative made positive life decisions and many embraced faith in Jesus Christ.

Out of the many teens that went through the program, two families come to mind. I remember when this spunky teenaged girl and her eleven-year old brother joined our program. She lived in the ghetto. After coming faithfully to the program for about a year, it seemed that almost every other night when we took this sister and brother home the police would be breaking up a domestic dispute between their parents. Eventually this young girl started bringing witchcraft books to the program. She started making statements about how she didn't believe in God because He allowed so much pain in the world. I knew she wasn't talking about the pain of the world. She was talking about the pain in her home. I told her I would be praying for her and that I knew what was going on in her home between her parents. She shook her head to say no, everything was fine. I told her I knew what she was going through because I had been there myself when

I was young. She started to cry as she went inside of the house. I know the pain and confusion that exist for such a young person when there is such turmoil in the home. The next day I had the opportunity to sit down with her family to intervene and talk about some of the problems. At the end of the discussion her family accepted Christ into their hearts. Soon this young teen, along with her mother and two brothers were going to church.

One of the goals of the program was to help teens learn and handle responsibility. Robby was a 13-year-old kid that didn't get into trouble. His mother signed him up for our program because he wasn't mature for his age. After some time I periodically received notes from his mom saying he was maturing and handling responsibility much better. One thing about Robby that troubled me was although he was a pretty good kid he didn't see his need for faith in Christ. Sometime after completing the program I received a call from him that I will never forget. He had received his learning permit to drive, and was getting straight A's in school. He saved the best news for last. He was now regularly attending church. Even better, his entire family was attending as well. That was great news. I told him I was proud of him and encouraged him to stick with it.

In addition to working directly with youth in our community through Youth Challenge, I had the opportunity to speak to thousands of people about teen issues, as well as about what Jesus Christ had done in my life. In Boise, Idaho I was interviewed on the radio and as a result won the best of show for the year. I was invited to speak for a station that aired in both Australia and New Zealand. I learned that there is a real problem with the Mafia in this part of the world. While in Idaho, Anne and I attended a private luncheon held for Dan Quayle, the Vice President of the United States, by the Idaho Family Forum, a non profit organization associated with Focus on the Family. After hearing Vice President Quale speak, we were able to meet him and had our picture taken with him as well.

  I was invited to speak on teen issues for Focus on the Family's radio program called Family News in Focus by the Focus Youth Culture Department. This taping aired worldwide. I was also invited to share my story with the Youth Culture Department of Focus on the Family. Fort Carson Army base invited me to speak to youth about staying away from drugs, gangs, and violence. I spoke to about 140 at-risk youth who had attended the summer camp for which I received the Commanders Award of Merit that was signed by the Major General of the Fort Carson Army Base, one of America's oldest and largest Army Bases. I keep this on my wall in my office. Finally, I was invited to take part in a meeting with the leaders of Promise Keeper's to help come up with a strategy to reach the youth attending the men's conferences with their dads. These were some of the wonderful opportunities I had to motivate others to a deeper faith in Christ and to encourage youth to make positive life decisions.

  After serving in Youth Challenge for seven years I felt it was time to bring Youth Challenge to a close. I continued the program long enough to allow the Lord to lead me back into the advertising field. My wife Anne told me about an opportunity to start an advertising company in Colorado. It was a display advertising company that placed advertising displays in high traffic areas. Anne and I met with the representative about the company, and then about a week or so later he called and asked us to meet him and an investor from Denver at a restaurant. I was introduced to Dan, a multi-millionaire originally from Arizona. He specialized in acquisitions and mergers of major insurance companies (that is buying and selling companies worth over one hundred million dollars). He made his millions in the information telephone business, you know, when you dial 411 to get a phone number from the Phone Company. Dan explained to us he was looking for individuals and couples to run the advertising company in various territories. After the meeting we got a call the next day and were told we had been selected. We were to meet Dan the next day to go over the paperwork and to pick up a check for ten thousand dollars to cover our pay and the supplies needed for the first month of operations. I was happy to be back in the advertising field.

    A new chapter of our lives had begun and Project Youth Challenge had come to an end. The last day with the teens came with sadness. We had a big pizza party for the youth. Afterward, I took the group home one by one. These were teens that had been in the program for a couple of years, the faithful ones. It all came together when I took the last teen home; his name was Chris. As Chris stepped out of the van, he stopped and turned to say, "Thanks Ron for Youth Challenge and for being there for us. It made a difference." I was so glad Chris had it in him to say that. Afterward, as I was driving away, the Lord Jesus spoke to my heart and said, "Well done, you did a great job." I thanked the Lord for allowing me to impact so many lives, and thanked Him for the impact these young ones had on my life as well.

    With hard work and the Lord's blessings I was able

to place the advertising displays in major malls and grocery stores. Part of the reason the major malls and grocery stores were willing to network with our company is because I was able to put together a sponsorship program for the local Salvation Army. The sponsorship included donating funds and using the advertising system to help raise much needed awareness, and support for the programs that the Salvation Army runs to help at-risk youth, families, and the elderly by providing them with shelter, clothing, food, and toys during the holidays. Companies started advertising on the displays.

  Dan called me after about the third month and told me he had just returned from a business trip in California, and that while on his flight on his way back he was thinking how impressed he was with how far we had taken the advertising company in our territory. He then asked if I would be his equal partner in his advertising company. We met and put together the paperwork for a Limited Liability Corporation where I was a corporate officer and an equal partner. I would receive a high salary each month along with a car allowance. I tried to hide my excitement in front of Dan; trying to maintain a level of professionalism, yet when I was at home I excitedly jumped up and down, thanking the Lord Jesus for His blessings.

  Sometime after forming the partnership, Dan and I bought out two magazines. One was a local coupon magazine; the other was a major computer publication that was being distributed statewide by the local news paper named The Gazette. The Gazette and the computer publication were owned by the same company that owns the Orange County Register, and the Press Enterprise of Riverside, both in California. I was now the Publisher for Peak Computing Magazine and the Peak Computing web site. Unknown to me, being a Publisher was a top position; some people made a big deal about meeting me. I played it down not making a big deal out of it. I gained a lot of great experience and my level of confidence as a professional grew. I worked with top computer firms and major Universities in Colorado. I worked with small and large ad agencies on advertising campaigns as well.

To top it all off my wife and I have been blessed with our fourth child. Natalie was born mid January of 2000. Natalie was healthy and I am told resembles her daddy. She was a beautiful baby with a full head of hair. We brought her home in the middle of winter when it was teeth chattering cold. I am so fortunate and thankful to be able to provide my children with a life I knew nothing about as a child. It is truly a season of blessings from the Lord.

Along with being the Publisher came a lot of responsibility and hard work. Finally, after about two years or so as Publisher, I decided to put my experience to work for Verizon as an Advertising Executive. Verizon is one of the largest publishing companies in the world. I was assigned to the Beverly Hills (think Hollywood), West Los Angeles, and Long Beach territories, beach communities in Southern California. I made the change because I wanted to have a healthier balance between my family and work, and I felt it was safe and good timing to move my family back to California. After sometime working as an Advertising Executive, I was recognized as one of the top Advertising Executives for the region, and number one in my office, maintaining a high level of success. My manager made the comment that she appreciated the fact that my family was one of my top priorities, yet at the same time I consistently performed well.

As a result of the Lord's direction and blessings in the advertising field, my wife and I were able to invest the resources we had into real estate. We have chosen to live in a modest brand new home in a brand new neighborhood in Southern California, and at the same time have invested money in other new homes as well. Without going into details, as a result of our investments, our real estate holdings are in the millions of dollars. I am deeply grateful to the Lord for his wonderful blessings, and I only share this aspect of my life to encourage young readers to see how positive life decisions and the power of faith can lead anybody to a good and safe life, and that dreams do still come true.

I have learned to count my blessings and to be optimistic about the future; however, to this day there are still difficulties in life to contend with. I still every once in a while have difficulty breathing because of asthma, although nothing close to when I was younger. My wife and I still have disagreements, and the children don't always want to cooperate (they are kids, what do you expect, right?) When things don't go smooth in life, say at work, or with family, I get discouraged and frustrated like anyone else, and perhaps because of my past, I am sometimes fearful of loosing everything I hold so dear. I take heart in knowing that Jesus Christ isn't done with me yet. His word says He will be faithful to complete the work He started in my life unto the day I go to meet my son Keith in heaven.

Christ walks with me daily and helps me to understand that He is near to help me through this rough and tumble "jungle" we call life. I certainly do not seek out difficulties, nor do I pretend they don't exist. Yes, Jesus wants to bless us with an abundant life in more ways than one; however, there is no escaping that along with life's ups, come downs, no matter who you are. Sickness, finances, difficult circumstances, and even death are no respecter of age, gender, wealth, or position. One of my favorite scriptures has always been John 16:33, "in the world you shall have troubles, but be of good cheer, for I have overcome the world". Jesus spoke those words, and they are as true today as the day He spoke them. As a result, when I come out of a difficult time I come out the better for it, having learned something, or having grown in some way. Hopefully having become more like Christ, having made the right decisions along with choosing to maintain a positive attitude in the midst of it all, although I do admit I am not always successful with the attitude part, even so I am improving. There have been times when I couldn't see or understand the why's, and it was during those times that Jesus held me the closest; all I could do was come to Him in prayer, lay my burdens at His feet, thank Him through praise and worship for the answers to my prayers, and trust that everything was going to be all right. As you have read, He has always come through in the end, even the times when it seemed I could not hold on any longer.

    Everyone has a great need within himself or herself to have purpose and meaning in this life, to make a mark, or a lasting impression. For me personally it is in knowing that because I wholeheartedly love my children I am making a mark in their hearts and minds for eternity by giving them the attention and time needed, along with endeavoring to be a faithful friend and a loving husband to my beautiful wife Anne. Most importantly, I am striving to maintain and increase my faith, love, and trust in God by spending time in a relationship with Jesus Christ through prayer, worship, and reading the Bible. As a result I have meaning and purpose. Take away my career in advertising, along with the material things, and all I am left with is my faith in Christ, along with a loving family, and yet still I have purpose and meaning in this life, and I believe this is the true meaning of the word success.

R.K. Jensen

AFTERWARD

Sometimes it is hard to count my blessings. I don't intend to think about the past, wishing somehow my childhood could have been better, yet as a result, I have come to realize that my experiences have helped to shape me and make me stronger. Because of my past I have had some tremendous opportunities to share my story with countless thousands of youngsters all across the world, as well as with adults from all walks of life. For that I am thankful and perhaps even more grateful as a result of my past for the many blessings God has chosen to bless me with.

Most recently, I have been a guest speaker for Teen Challenge, and at local churches. The young men going through Teen Challenge have shared with me that it is motivating and inspiring to hear a young man such as myself speak about the importance of faith and family, and about the blessings the Lord has given me through hard work and obtaining an education, mostly because I have been where they are. Hearing that kind of response is rewarding, encouraging, and motivates me to press on in my faith.

I am learning that God loves to bless his children with more than their needs, sometimes choosing to bless us with forgotten dreams. As a child I had excelled in the visual arts and was told that I would do well in advertising. I had actually forgotten about that until recently when I was thinking about how well I had done as a top Advertising Executive for a large corporation. It was during this time as an Advertising Executive that I remembered a childhood dream of one day becoming an actor. Not necessarily a famous actor, just someone who acts on stage and if I am lucky enough, on television as well. I decided to do something about it and took some acting lessons at the same acting school Helen Hunt received her training. The Director is a sweet and very sharp woman of faith named Dorothy. She is a film actress from the early days of Hollywood. She was in the Wizard of Oz, she danced on film with Fred Astair, she was practically related to Joan Crawford, friends with the legendary Bob Hope, and was in Gone with the Wind. She is an inspiration to me and my children, along with those at the Academy who encouraged me in my acting and writing, (such as Cathy, Bob, Wayne, and Judianna; I cannot forget about the great friendship and encouragement of Dr. Sanders and her family along with the many trips to Disneyland).

As a result of the training I was able to act on stage and I actually landed a couple of roles on National Television. The first role I did was a Western Documentary called *Clay County War* that aired internationally on NBC's the History Channel. This was filmed at the Paramount Studios Old West Ranch near Hollywood. I was cast in a lead role, and did some stunt work on the film. After the first day of filming I was asked by the Producer whether or not the Director had told me that I would be hanging by the neck from the gallows on the next day of filming. It was news to me! The Producers had authentic gallows built on the set (gallows are basically the wooden platform with a trap door used to hang people by the neck back in the Old West days). During the filming my neck was placed in a real noose made of rope, then the Cowboy holding the cord to the trap door pulled the cord, releasing the trap door underneath me. I literally fell through the door, and was hanging by a rope around my neck. So it appeared. I was actually wearing a mountain climber's harness underneath my western outfit. The harness was connected to a steel cable that was threaded through the rope that lead to a support beam above my head. It looked pretty real on television.

    The second movie I did was as a background actor in a film called Peter the Rock. I am in several scenes. We filmed at different locations, including an authentic Castle. This also aired as recently as Easter of 2003 on the History Channel. I enjoyed acting on film in Hollywood along with performing in theatre productions with others in the acting industry who have been on shows such as Zoey 101, Crocodile Dundee (part one), Malcolm in the Middle, Allie McBeal, Judging Amy, General Hospital, and Lizzie McGuire, among others. I have also had the tremendous opportunity to share my story with some of the actors and directors I worked with in Hollywood. One of the more successful actresses commented that she was really inspired by my story. The actors and actresses were very receptive and even encouraged me to make this book happen. I was taken back when my son Seth and I got to work with Helen Hunt's mom on a series of photographs. She had pictures of Helen from when she was just a kid, and I could see the Hollywood sign from her front window. She took the picture of me that appears in the last chapter of this book titled, "Keynotes". My acting friends, as well as the folks I met at Focus on the Family, have encouraged me to turn my story into a movie. As a result I am working with industry film professionals who want to make this happen, and I am currently working on the screenplay for the movie. Prayerfully this will take place so that many others will be encouraged as a result of seeing the film.

In closing I would like to say it has been with a grateful heart that I have shared with you the many hardships and trials God has miraculously delivered me from, along with the wonderful blessings God has granted me. Indeed my life has been filled with extraordinary events and circumstances, yet, when I consider that I should have died of my bullet and stab wounds at the young age of fourteen, only to live to be able to have a family of my own, and the opportunity to be a part of their lives, along with a faith in Christ, I am deeply grateful to Jesus Christ for reaching out to me when I was left for dead in that cold, lonely-dark field so many years ago, adopting me as His own, and giving me a future, and a hope. May you realize your dreams, and the true fulfillment that comes from a deep found faith in and relationship with Jesus Christ.

✵ R.K. Jensen ✵

EPILOGUE

I will bless the LORD at all times;
   His praise shall continually be in my mouth.
My soul will make its boast in the LORD;
   The humble will hear it and rejoice.
O magnify the LORD with me,
   And let us exalt His name together.
I sought the LORD, and He answered me,
   And delivered me from all my fears.
And we know that all things work together for good
to those who love God
   To those who are the called according to His purpose.
O fear the LORD, you His saints;
   For to those who fear Him there is no want.
The young lions do lack and suffer hunger;
   But they who seek the LORD shall not be in want of
   any good thing.
Neither death nor life, nor angels nor principalities nor
any other created thing,
   Shall be able to separate us from the love of God
   which is in Christ Jesus our Lord.
The righteous cry, and the LORD hears
   And delivers them out of all their troubles.
The LORD is near to the brokenhearted
   And saves those who are crushed in spirit.
Many are the afflictions of the righteous,
   But the LORD delivers him out of them all.

Psalm 34:1-4; 9,10; 17-19
Romans 8:28, 38

Keynotes
Interviews, Speaking, and Workshops

Publisher and Author R.K. Jensen speaks to assemblies of youth, parents, and youth workers about avoiding the pitfalls of the urban/gang culture, and the importance of dreams, goals, staying positive, overcoming obstacles, the great value of positive role models/mentors, and being strong minded in the face of the great pressures young people face today. R.K. Jensen also shares his dramatic story with church assemblies and youth groups about the power of faith, God's amazing grace and miracle working power in the face of the most impossible and darkest circumstances, helping people of faith to gain a deeper understanding of a more personal relationship with Jesus Christ, strengthening their trust and faith in Jesus Christ, and understanding that God has a wonderful plan for each one of our lives.

R.K. Jensen has been recognized as guest speaker of the year for radio broadcasts and has received various awards and honors for his speaking, such as the Commanding Generals Award of Merit from the Fort Carson Army Base in Colorado (Camp Red Devil Youth-at-Risk Outreach). Officers of the U.S. Army stated that it was the best youth presentation they have seen or heard. R.K. Jensen had the honor of being a guest speaker for Focus on the Family's Pastoral Ministries department and was said to be Focus on the Family's official authority on Youth-at risk and gang issues, and was invited to speak on youth issues for the

☙ R.K. Jensen ❧

Family News in Focus radio program, which aired World-wide. R.K. Jensen was the featured guest of the radio program Balance Point in Idaho. The broadcast was later voted best show of the year. Sometime thereafter, R.K. Jensen and his wife attended a private luncheon with then Vice President of the United States Dan Quale. R.K. Jensen has been a guest speaker for Teen Challenge of Southern California. The men were encouraged in their decision to break the bonds of drugs, gangs, and alcohol. A young resident of Teen Challenge named Ian commented that it gave him great hope and encouragement to see someone living a successful life who had grown up with the same rough circumstances he had. Other Teen Challenge residents made similar comments. Promise Keepers invited R.K. Jensen along with prominent youth leaders throughout the United States to a special planning session to reach the young men and boys attending the Promise Keepers conferences with their fathers. Most recently R.K. has spoken in Jails and Juvenile Halls with various ministries, such as Youth For Christ. R.K.'s dramatic story has aired throughout the world on the radio, including the United States of America, New Zealand, and Australia.

For complete information on interviewing or speaking inquiries please send or email your request to the Publisher:

Aaron Communications III
Re: R.K. Jensen
PO Box 63270
Colorado Springs, CO 80962-3270

Email: aaroncom3rkjensen@yahoo.com

FREE BOOKS FOR YOUNG PEOPLE

A special request from R.K. Jensen

"There are thousands of young boys and girls, young men and women, who will not be able to purchase this book, yet would greatly benefit from reading *Left for Dead - Faith, Family, and the Mob*. The most common response I have received from young people who have read my book or have heard me speak is they are greatly encouraged and visibly touched because I personally know firsthand the pain and struggles that they themselves live with day in and day out, and seeing someone like myself succeeding in life gives them great hope and courage for a future. Please read a portion of a letter I received from a United States Marine who was a Prisoner of War; his is an honest and touching response to my story. An intro of his letter appears at the beginning of this book.

Will you please join me in bringing this message of hope to youth and young adults here in America and around the World? You can help youth by sending any dollar amount you believe would help. Please join me by sponsoring youth by providing them with a copy of my inspirational true story.

The books are sent at no charge to organizations such as children's hospitals, orphanages, foster care facilities, summer camps, inner-city youth outreach, churches, juvenile halls, and prisons.

R.K. Jensen

Please understand there are hard costs associated with publishing, especially printing and distribution costs. Your sponsorship will help deliver FREE books to the one's who need them the most. Thank you for your help, and please pray for this worthy effort."

R.K. Jensen

Sponsorship Bonus: Receive two copies of *Left for Dead - Faith, Family, & the Mob*, for $20.00. One copy is a personally signed copy for yourself or as a gift (mailed free to your address), and the second copy will be donated to the Youth Sponsorship program.

SPONSOR ONLINE:
http://www.aaroncom3.com/sponsorTeen.html

Number of youth sponsored:_____ x 8.00 = $_____
Sponsorship 2 Book bonus:_____ x $20.00 = $_____
Person to receive signed copy:_____
Name: _____ Telephone: _____
Email address: _____
Address: _____
City: _____ State: _____ Zip: _____

Method of sponsorship: Check__ Money Order __
(Payable to Aaron Communications III, memo line: youth sponsorship)
    Credit Card __: Visa __ Master Card __ AMEX __ Disc __
Card Number:_____ Code on reverse: _____
Name on Card:_____ Exp date:_____

Please supply above information and mail to:
Aaron Communications III
Youth Sponsorship
P.O. Box 63270, Colorado Springs, CO 80962

ೞ LEFT FOR DEAD - FAITH, FAMILY, & THE MOB ೞ

Order a gift copy at a reduced price

Indicate choice: Soft Cover:___ Hard Cover:___ Quantity:_____
Price for one book: $11.95, soft cover. $19.95, hard cover.
Sales Tax: add 7% for orders shipped to Colorado addresses.
Special Quantity discount: Take $2.00 off for each book ordered for any quantity over two books. Quantity discount good on direct orders from publisher only. Your local bookstore or online bookstore may have special offers available.

Shipping charges for all gift orders:
U.S.A.: $4.00 for first book, and $2.00 for each additional.
International: $9.00 for first book, and $5 for each additional.

Person to receive signed copy:_____
Name: _____ Telephone: _____
Email address: _____
Address: _____
City: _____ State: _____ Zip: _____

Method of payment: Check__ Money Order __
(Payable to Aaron Communications III, memo line: youth sponsorship)
Credit Card __: Visa __ Master Card __ AMEX __ Disc __
Card Number:_____ Code on reverse: _____
Name on Card:_____ Exp date:_____

ORDER ONLINE:

http://www.aaroncom3.com/books.html

APPENDIX A

God's plan for Salvation

God loves each one of us so much that He has made a way for us to spend all of eternity with Him in heaven. The Bible clearly explains how to receive eternal life. I have put together some Bible verses about God's plan to explain how you can be totally sure you are going to heaven.

1. We need to recognize that we all have sin in our lives, small or great, there is no difference. It isn't about how good we are, or how religious one might be. We all have sinned one way or another.

- Romans 3:10

"As it is written, there is none righteous, no, not one."

- Ecclestiastes 7:20

"For there is not a just man upon earth, that doeth good, and sinneth not."

- Romans 3:23

"For all have sinned, and come short of the glory of God."

2. There is a price to pay for sin. No matter how small or great the sin, there is a consequence. The consequence is eternal separation from God for all eternity. The good news is that God does not want for you or me to pay that penalty. He has made a way to have the penalty for sin (death) paid in full.

- Romans 6:23

"For the wages of sin is death, but the gift of God is eternal life through Jesus Christ our Lord."

- Revelation 21:8

"But the fearful, and unbelieving, and the abominable, and murderers, and whoremongers, and sorcerers, and idolaters, and all liars, shall have their part in the lake which burneth with fire and brimstone: which is the second death."

3. Jesus willingly paid the price for our sin with His death on the Cross. A death He did nothing to deserve. God is not willing that any should pay that price, so He sent His Son in our place. Simply put, God in His love, made a way for all peoples to receive complete forgiveness for all of their sins, and thereby receive the free gift of eternal salvation through faith in Jesus, the Son of God.

- Romans 5:8

"But God commendeth his love toward us, in that while we were yet sinners, Jesus died for us."

- 1 Corinthians 15:8

"For I delivered unto you first of all that which I also received, how that Jesus died for our sins according to the scriptures;"

4. King David was said to be a great man of faith, even though King David made some terrible mistakes in his adult life as ruler of Israel. King David wholeheartedly repented of his errors and trusted God to forgive him. He truly turned away from his wrong doing, and trusted God. God did forgive him, and called King David His friend, a man after God's own heart. In the same way,

when you and I repent by turning away from practicing sin, as we place our trust in God's Son Jesus and His death on the Cross, God will indeed forgive our sins.

- Luke 13:3

"I tell you, Nay: but, except ye repent, ye shall all likewise perish."

- Isaiah 55:7

"Let the wicked forsake his way, and the unrighteous man his thoughts: and let him return unto the Lord, and he will have mercy upon him; and to our God, for he will abundantly pardon."

- Acts 20:21

"Testifying both to the Jews, and also to the non-Jews, repentance toward God, and faith toward our Lord Jesus Christ."

5. Many people make the mistake of trying to earn salvation. Such as by trying to do good deeds, or by being a good person, or through some religious act. Salvation is a FREE gift from God. We in no way earn or deserve eternal salvation. We are only deserving of the penalty of our sins, eternal damnation, the second death. Yet, Jesus paid the price for our sins. He died an innocent man, so that when we put our faith in Him, His death counts as payment for our sins. God the Father raised Jesus from the dead, sealing the deal to promise to forgive all that put their trust in Jesus. That is God's plan, He has done the work, we receive salvation freely.

- Romans 6:23

"For the wages of sin is death, but the **gift** of God is eternal life through Jesus Christ our Lord."

- Ephesians 2:8-9

"For by grace are ye saved through faith; and that not of yourselves: it is the gift of God: Not of works, lest any man should boast."

- Titus 3:4-6

"But after that the kindness and love of God our Savior toward man appeared, Not by works of righteousness which we have done, but according to his mercy he saved us, by the washing of regeneration, and renewing of the Holy Ghost; Which he shed on us abundantly through Jesus Christ our Savior;"

- Romans 11:6

"And if by grace, then is it no more of works: otherwise grace is no more grace. But if it be of works, then is it no more grace: otherwise work is no more work."

6. God's gift to the world is His Son Jesus. You will never be disappointed when you put your trust in Him. God keeps His word. He will not let you down. This is the greatest gift a person could ever receive, forgiveness of sin, the promise of eternal life, and best of all, the open door to have a lasting friendship with the God of Creation.

- John 3:16

"For God so loved the world, that he gave his only begotten Son, that whosoever believes in him should not perish, but have everlasting life."

- Romans 10:13

"For whosoever shall call upon the name of the Lord shall be saved."

- John 1:12

"But as many as received him (Jesus Christ), to them gave he power to become the sons of God, even to them that believe on his name:"

- 1 John 5:13

"These things have I written unto you that believe on the name of the Son of God; that ye may know that ye have eternal life, and that ye may believe on the name of the Son of God."

- Romans 10:9-11

"That if thou shalt confess with thy mouth the Lord Jesus, and shalt believe in thine heart that God hath raised Him from the dead, thou shalt be saved. For with the heart man believes unto righteousness; and with the mouth confession is made unto salvation. For the Scripture saith, Whosoever believes on Him shall not be ashamed."

7. The thief who died on the cross next to Jesus simply said, "Lord, when you enter into your Kingdom, remember me." Jesus responded, "this day you will be with me in Paradise" (Luke 23). The thief received eternal salvation and that day entered Paradise simply because he believed and acted on that belief. The thief did not have to wait to be saved until after he mended his ways, or cleaned up his life. In the same way, none of us has to wait to "clean up our act", or to make amends before we too can be saved. A simple act of repentance and acting out your faith is all that is needed to receive this most precious gift of eternal salvation. God has made it simple.

2 Corinthians 6:2
...for He (Jesus) says, "At the acceptable time I listened to you,

And on the day of salvation I helped you"; behold, now is "the acceptable time," behold, now is "the day of salvation"

Revelation 3:20
"Behold, I stand at the door, and knock, if any man hear my voice and open the door, I will come in to him, and will eat with him, and he with me."

Luke 23: 39
One of the criminals who were hanged railed at him, saying, "Are you not the Christ? Save yourself and us!" 40 But the other rebuked him, saying, "Do you not fear God, since you are under the same sentence of condemnation? 41 And we indeed justly; for we are receiving the due reward of our deeds; but this man has done nothing wrong." 42 And he said, "Jesus, remember me when you come into your kingdom." 43 And he said to him, "Truly, I say to you, today you will be with me in Paradise."

To receive God's free gift of eternal life please pray to God this simple prayer:

"Dear Jesus, I believe that you are the Son of God, that you died on the cross for my sins, and that on the third day you rose from the grave. I admit that I am a sinner, and I need your forgiveness. Please forgive me for all of my sins. Please come into my heart, and fill my soul with your peace, and love. Thank you Lord for dying for my sins, and for giving me your gift of eternal salvation. Please help me in my new relationship with you. In Jesus' name. Amen"

If you prayed this prayer I would like to be the first to say, "Congratulations, and welcome to the family of God."

You can now be one hundred percent certain that you are going to heaven for eternity. You can be certain that you belong to Jesus. You are a child of God. You have full rights and privileges as a child of the Most High God. Yes, it is that simple. Believe, ask, and receive. That is it. It doesn't matter if you don't feel anything inside. It is a fact that you are saved.

The Journey has just begun. Helpful steps to building your faith in Jesus.

I took that first step in 1981, in a church in Southern California. My faith in Christ has developed into a relationship that has lasted through the years; in part because I took some very important steps to make sure that my new found faith took root, and grew into a mature, close relationship. As with any relationship, or friendship, it takes some effort on both parts to grow close. The scripture James 4:8 "Draw near to God and he will draw near to you", meant a lot to me when I first accepted Christ. I learned that as my understanding grew about Jesus the Christ, and Jesus the person, I grew closer to Him, and He in turn grew closer to me. The scripture also says that the more we know Jesus, the more He is able, (and willing) to bless us. All the effort is not on your shoulders. It is not a hard thing to grow to know Jesus as your personal Lord and Savior.

To help you grow in your new found faith, I have outlined some simple, helpful steps. These steps outlined are tried and true, and best of all, based on scripture found in the Bible. God bless you on your new journey. These steps start on the next page.

❧ LEFT FOR DEAD - FAITH, FAMILY, & THE MOB ☙

1. TELL SOMEONE ABOUT YOUR NEW FAITH.

It is okay if you are shy, however, this is great news. Tell someone you can trust, such as a close relative or friend. You may be very nervous or scared, that is perfectly normal. Here are a couple of scriptures to motivate you.

Romans 10:9 - That if thou shalt confess with thy mouth the Lord Jesus, and shalt believe in thine heart that God hath raised him from the dead, thou shalt be saved.

Romans 10:10 - For with the heart man believes unto righteousness; and with the mouth confession is made unto salvation.

2. BEGIN READING THE BIBLE

The word of God is food for the Spirit. As you grow in your correct knowledge of Jesus, so does your Spirit within. You become stronger in your faith.
The Bible states in Romans 10:17 - So then faith comes by hearing, and hearing by the word of God.

The Bible also states in Matthew 4:4 - "It is written, 'Man shall not live by bread alone, but by every word that proceeds from the mouth of God.'"

A good book to start with is the book of John in the new testament of the Bible. Then continue on until you get to the book of Revelation. I would suggest reading at least 3 chapters per day. Begin and end each reading session with a short word of prayer, asking the Lord for understanding.

The important thing is to read with understanding. You don't have to feel like you need to read the Bible in one year. Take your time to learn and comprehend each story and teaching. Read it like you read a letter from a dear friend, hanging on every word. After all, the Bible is God's personal letter to you.

If you do not have a Bible, and you are online, you can visit www.bible.com and read the bible for free.

3. ATTENDING CHURCH/FELLOWSHIP

Acts 2:42 - And they (the believers) devoted themselves to the apostles' teaching and fellowship, to the breaking of bread and the prayers.

Hebrews 10:25 - Not forsaking the assembling of ourselves together, as the manner of some is; but exhorting one another: and so much the more, as ye see the day approaching.

The important thing is to find a Bible believing church. Which is nothing more than the gathering of people with like minded beliefs. The purpose of the church is to help people grow in their faith and understanding of God. To come together as a group to praise God, and to strengthen and encourage one another in the faith.

You can usually find a listing of churches in your yellow pages, or in the religion section of the Saturday edition of your local news paper. Perhaps a friend or close relative of yours goes to a Bible believing church. They would be most happy to have you as their guests.

When you do go, ask about a new believer's class. Not only will you learn a lot about your faith, you will also get to know new people like yourself, as well as some of the staff from the church.

Some of the Denominations that I am aware of that have healthy views on the Bible are:

Southern Baptist, Assembly of God, Nazarene, Calvary Chapel, and Missionary Alliance, among others. There are many non denominational churches as well, I just wanted to give you a starting point if you are unaware of a church to attend. A brief word of caution, there are some churches that have their own version of the Bible, and have misinterpreted the Scriptures. Either by adding books to the Bible or simply twisting the meaning of sound scripture. These religions are Jehovah Witnesses, Mormons (Church of Jesus Christ of Latter Day Saints), and Religious Science. There are others, however, these are the closest to true Christianity and can easily confuse a new believer, so I want you to be aware so you are not misled.

There are a lot of religions in the world, however, Jesus said "no man comes unto the Father but by Me." He is the only true way to heaven, consequently, it is very important to go to a church with an accurate view of the Bible.

4. PRAYER AND PRAISE

Matthew 11:28-30 "Come unto me, all that labour and are heavy laden, and I will give you rest. Take my yoke upon you, and learn of me; for I am meek and lowly in heart: and ye shall find rest unto your souls. For my yoke is easy, and my burden is light."

When we spend time in prayer and reading of the word, it is good to offer praise and thanksgiving to the Lord for the great things He has done for us. He is truly worthy. It helps to set a time aside sometime during the day when you can be alone.

When life brings along a trying time, as it often does, praising the Lord has a way of making everything okay. In the book of Job, in the Old Testament, we learn of a man named Job who endured severe hardship in his life. There came a pivotal point in his life when he realized, compared to the greatness of God, how small his severe trials really were. Not that they didn't matter, or that they weren't valid concerns, only in that when he turned his focus away from his trials, and set his eyes upon the Lord, he realized that God's ability to work things out for the good, was greater than any problem he could face.

Romans 8:28 - We know that in everything God works for good with those who love him, who are called according to his purpose.

Even though we may get discouraged, because of our relationship with Christ, we know that everything will work out for the good. True praise from the heart is strength to your soul. There are the times when I praise Him just because. Everything seems fine in my life, and I just want to praise Him to say thanks, and that He is worthy. Then there are the times when I really don't feel up to praising the Lord. It is at those times that we offer up a sacrifice of praise. Usually, after I have praised Him, I understand what it was I was bothered about and I am then able to talk to the Lord about it. In the end, I feel much better.

Hebrews 13:15 - By him therefore let us offer the sacrifice of praise to God continually, that is, the fruit of our lips giving thanks to his name.

So go on and praise the Lord. Allow His peace to flood your soul.

5. GOD'S GARDEN

There was a time in my Christianity that I became impatient with myself in relation to putting into practice the very things I have written about. Nothing came easy. I certainly didn't feel like I was growing as fast as the people in the Bible must have. It wasn't until years later that I learned that growing in Christ is a process that takes years.

What I learned was that the Apostle Paul spent about twelve years in the desert, working a trade, growing with fellow believers, and growing in his relationship with Christ. After receiving Christ, he did not immediately get it right, and go into ministry. It took time. A lot of time.

In the same way that a gardener tends to his garden over a time and a season, so too God gives us the time and attention we need to grow and mature. God is patient, likewise, be patient with yourself and give it time.

Philippians 1:6 - And I am sure that he who began a good work in you will bring it to completion at the day of Jesus Christ.

R.K. Jensen

PASS IT ON

If you were encouraged by my story, and have benefited from it, I would like to request for you to tell a friend or relative about my book. My only hope is that people from all walks of life will be inspired and touched by this message. Once again, thank you so very much for reading my story.

R.K. Jensen

QUESTIONS OR CONCERNS

I welcome your comments or questions.

Please write to me by mailing any letters to the publisher or you can e-mail me direct:

aaroncom3rkjensen@yahoo.com

Aaron Communications III
Attention: R.K. Jensen
P.O. Box 63270
Colorado Springs, CO 80962

INSPIRATIONAL ART BY R.K. JENSEN

View hand drawn images depicting a modern vision of God in the clouds. Go online with absolutely no charge to read the story and to view the art. People from all over the world have enjoyed this inspirational art by award winning artist R.K. Jensen. People from such countries as the U.S.A., Australia (top two countries), India, Canada, Great Britain, the European Union, China, Germany, the Netherlands, Singapore, Sweden, Hong Kong, Spain, the Czech Republic, Belgium, the Philippines, New Zealand, Norway, Japan, Turkey, Switzerland, as well as Kenya, and the list is growing every day.

http://www.imagesofGod.net/html/home.htm

Portrait of Jesus; King of Kings ©2003

ॐ R.K. Jensen ॐ

Four Living Creatures in the Throne Room of God ©2003

4 Horsemen; breaking the Seals of the Scrolls ©2003